Eric Clapton

The Illustrated Disco/Biography
by Marc Roberty & Chris Welch

Omnibus Press
London/New York/Sydney/Cologne

©Copyright 1984 Omnibus Press
(A division of Book Sales Limited).
Book designed by Karen Fenton.
Typeset by Capital Setters, London W1.
Printed in England by Anchor Brendon
Ltd, Tiptree, Essex.

ISBN 0.7119.0526.6
UK Order No. OP 42993
Cherry Lane Order No. 67084

Exclusive distributors:

Book Sales Limited
78 Newman Street, London W1P 3LA. UK.

Omnibus Press
GPO Box 3304. Sydney. NSW 2001.
Australia.

Cherry Lane Books
P.O. Box 430,
Port Chester,
NY 10573,
New York, U.S.A.

Hello and thank you to the following:
Mark Lewkowicz, Simon Bell, Mike
Sawin, Mal Barker, Bob Graig, Jared
Houser, Carol Norris, Howard Mylett,
Tina Cook, Steve Margo, Stuart Pearsell,
Bruce Lawson, Guy and Mady Roberty.

A big thank you to Diane Harris for her
typing.

Thanks to Chris Charlesworth for his
excellent editing.

Thanks to photographer Barry Plummer.

Photo Credits: Barry Plummer (pages 4, 8,
12 & 80), Marc Roberty (pages 15 & 29),
Steve Emberton (page 70).

FOR ERIC CLAPTON.

CONTENTS

ERIC CLAPTON
A SHORT BIOGRAPHY
BY CHRIS WELCH

Eric Clapton, best loved of all the great rock guitarists, has enjoyed a twenty year recording career and produced a volume of consistently fine performances. Whatever changes and crises have occurred in his personal life, Clapton the musician has always stood firm by his musical beliefs. This has sometimes led to uncompromising or even perverse decisions. And yet, whenever he has changed bands, styles or direction, he has invariably been proved right, however long it has taken audiences to catch up.

Clapton, guitarist, singer and composer, has been a source of inspiration to countless young players since he first emerged on the British blues scene back in 1964. He was the first wholly convincing white blues virtuoso, and after early experience with such bands as The Yardbirds and John Mayall's Blues Breakers, went on to define heavy rock in Cream. He was a key figure in the small army of British talent that cross-pollinated with their American counterparts to forge the concept of 'rock' as a living, progressive form, open to all kinds of influences.

A shy, sensitive and private person, he can easily be hurt and influenced by others, yet his inner strength and sense of humour delights in the absurd and takes comfort from the everyday world. He has often chosen to retreat from fame and commercial success to hide away as an anonymous worker. He likes to describe himself as 'a musical labourer'. It's a genuine enough facet of his character, but is also part of his ability to submerge himself into a role, a skill which as a young man enabled him to act out the part of a bluesman until he quite legitimately became one, accepted by the sternest critics. At the core of

Eric's success and appeal has always been an innate feeling for the blues.

He was born in Ripley, Surrey, on March 30, 1945. He went to Ripley Primary School and St. Bede's Secondary Modern before enrolling at Kingston School Of Art to study stained glass design. His father was a plasterer and bricklayer with little interest in music; nor had his mother though she took a keen interest in her son's career and kept an eye on everything that was written about him, often ringing reporters to correct mistakes.

His parents gave Eric his first guitar at the age of 15, after he discovered a blues album by Big Bill Broonzy. "I'd never heard anything like it," he recalled later. But he found playing guitar much harder than he thought and virtually gave up trying for two years. His parents thought it was just another craze to be quickly forgotten. But when he went to the art school he heard records owned by fellow students; the music of B.B. King, Muddy Waters, Chuck Berry, Robert Johnson and a favourite rocker, Buddy Holly.

The sudden upsurge of interest in blues among English youth was felt most keenly in the art colleges and replaced a previous preoccupation with traditional jazz. Eric was among those who didn't just want to play the records: he resurrected the old guitar and began practising. The next obvious step was to join a band and he played with his friend Tom McGuinness (who later went on to fame with Manfred Mann) in his first group The Roosters. It was 1963 and Eric was 18 years old. They played on the pub and party circuit around Richmond where they made plenty of friends, even if they didn't earn much money. The Roosters crowed from January to

September and were later acknowledged as one of the first regular British R&B groups. Eric also occasionally sat in with fellow pioneers Alexis Korner's Blues Incorporated at their Ealing Club.

When The Roosters broke up, Tom and Eric joined a band led by Liverpool singer Casey Jones called The Engineers. But Eric had become a blues purist and Casey Jones was too much of a pop singer. "I couldn't stand that for very long," he said. He stayed only a couple of weeks. As he had devoted more and more time to music and less to stained glass Eric was eventually expelled from the art college but by now the guitar dominated his life. He taught himself to play by listening to Chuck Berry and Bo Diddley records and delved into the history of rock'n'roll and its jazz, blues and gospel roots, For a while he played very much in a Chuck Berry vein before coming under the spell of the more melodic and sophisticated B.B. King and the Chicago blues players. Said Eric: "I knew after a while I had to develop my own style. I would do something I'd heard on record and then add something of my own. Gradually more of my own stuff took over."

Eric learned how to bend strings to alter notes and develop a 'singing' quality. To facilitate this he used very light strings which meant that he broke at least two on each number. While he patiently re-strung his guitar, audiences would begin a good-natured slow handclap – hence his nickname 'Slowhand' Clapton.

A fellow blues purist was guitarist Brian Jones who sometimes played with Eric and Tom. He went off to form The Rolling Stones who played a residency at the Richmond Crawdaddy Club. When The Stones outgrew the club and achieved pop fame, another local group, The Yardbirds took their place and soon won their own fan following. The leader of The Yardbirds was frail singer Keith Relf who had known Eric at art school, and once tentatively talked about forming a group with him.

The band's original guitarist Anthony 'Top' Topham was a pioneer blues enthusiast who found the role of lead guitarist too demanding. He also experienced parental opposition and when he quit Keith phoned Clapton to ask him down for a rehearsal. He arrived at the South Western Hotel and immediately fitted in with the band's musical policy. More than that, he was much further advanced as a guitarist and knew many more numbers than his predecessor. Clapton's arrival gave the band a huge boost.

The Yardbirds were managed by the emotional and enthusiastic Giorgio Gomelsky who ran the Crawdaddy Club and was a great jazz and blues fan. He was a Russian with a Swiss passport and seemed just the larger than life character to push the callow suburban youths into realising their potential. It was his ambition to make The Yardbirds as successful as The Stones, but it was not a policy that endeared itself to Eric.

In the first year or so with The Yardbirds Eric enjoyed the fact he could make a living as a musician and be presented as their star soloist. His reputation spread even more rapidly as fans travelled miles to see the group at the early Richmond jazz festivals or to the Marquee Club in Soho. There the atmosphere was electric as the band developed their 'rave up' style with increasing tempos and block chords. Eric's rhythm guitar style was particularly effective on 'Smokestack Lightning' and he soloed with burning power on 'I Wish You Would'. Evidence of the atmosphere at a live gig can be heard on the live session recorded at the Marquee in March 1964. 'I Wish You Would' (studio version) was released as the band's first single in June 1964.

The full line up of The Yardbirds included Eric, Keith, Paul Samwell-Smith (bass), Jim McCarty (drums) and Chris Dreja (rhythm guitar) who became particularly close to Eric.

In December 1963 the band recorded their first official album, also live at the Crawdaddy Club, but it was not released until a couple of years later. It featured the extra vocal talents of a genuine American blues man, the legendary Sonny Boy Williamson, who came to live and work in England. He regarded his enthusiastic backing group as "my boys". On the night of the recording session, Sonny Boy drank copious draughts of whiskey which didn't help the quality of the music. A set featuring The Yardbirds alone from the same night later appeared, somewhat mysteriously, on a Spanish LP in 1982.

The Yardbirds grew increasingly popular but they wanted to move on from hard-core blues into experiments with songwriting and recording techniques. Eric never shared this boyish enthusiasm for the future Yardbirds. He remained something of an enigma as far as the rest were concerned. When the band wore long hair, he trimmed his short. While the others smiled engagingly in photographs, he would look moody and sullen. He was constantly changing his image. Chris Dreja was not surprised to find that his room mate was very fond of the chameleon, a lizard that can change colour. At one stage Eric wore gay bouffant hair styles and Mod gear. Then he'd revert to sombre beatnik garb.

He was shy about his guitar playing and at first wouldn't take any solos, tending instead to try and hide behind his amplifier. But as his technique improved, so did his confidence.

The first time I met Eric was with The Yardbirds in a Fleet Street coffee bar. They were generally noisy and upset the waitresses. Eric, however, was quiet, softly spoken, with an amused smile. Their main concern was that the band might lose its hard core blues fans if 'Good Morning Little Schoolgirl' was a big hit. It wasn't. Soon after this initial encounter I went to see Eric playing with The Yardbirds at the Bromel Club in Bromley, Kent, and spoke to him after the usually exciting version of 'Smokestack Lightning' had gone down to minimal applause from a crowd more interested in the bar than the bandstand "You look fed up," I said. "You noticed," said Eric with heavy irony. Not long after, he quit the group.

Said Eric: "I was fooled into joining the group. I fooled myself, attracted by the pop thing, the big money, the travelling around and the little chicks. It wasn't until I had been doing it for eighteen months that I started to take my music seriously. I realised that I wanted to be doing it for the rest of my life, so I had better start doing it right."

The Yardbirds tied Eric down musically. They tried to rein in guitar solos which became increasingly violent and provoked more excitement in the audience than Keith's harmonica which generally dominated their recordings. It was odd that the band which became known as the nursery for some of the loudest, most extrovert guitarists, Clapton, Jeff Beck and Jimmy Page, should have been seen as a disciplinary force. But Eric would show just how much more he had to offer when he joined his next band.

"The Yardbirds were tying me down," he said later. "I wanted to get a step further on and they wanted more and more discipline. I was all screwed up about my playing and didn't like anything I did."

The crunch came with a record called 'For Your Love' which featured bongoes and a harpsichord. Eric hated it, and quit just before the record was released in March 1965.

There followed a confused period during which Eric was the subject of much rumour. He became an increasingly mysterious and much

idolised figure. He was invited by John Mayall to join The Bluesbreakers who specialised in the kind of 'pure' blues The Yardbirds had apparently abandoned. But Eric stayed for only a short time. He was still restless and envied his art school mates who led disorganised, Bohemian lives. He put together a group called The Glands and set off on a "trip round the world" which actually got as far as Greece. They ran out of funds and Eric came back to England to rejoin The Bluesbreakers. There was an audible sigh of relief on the English club scene.

His second stint with The Bluesbreakers ran from November 1965 through to June 1966. During this period hero worship grew to the extent that fans began to call him 'God' and there were cries of "Give God a solo" at gigs, while on city walls appeared the slogan 'Clapton is God.' I went to see Eric play with John Mayall during this period at a club in Putney (where I also saw The Byrds play a rare London gig). By this time Eric looked menacing, almost unapproachable in hairy sideboards and heavy blue denim. But he proved to be polite and I was lucky enough to hear him playing at the peak of his pure blues period.

The album he produced with Mayall in 1966 is a fine reminder of this period (Decca LK 4804). For many Clapton fans it still represents his best work.

Eric's guitar seems to fly with an exultant glee, and a breezy confidence that is infectious and heart warming. In the days before so many blues phrases had been turned into unwelcome clichés by dozens of mediocre 'blues bands' there was the added thrill of hearing something that seemed so much more authentic and exciting than the gauche rock and roll styles that prevailed. Overnight groups like The Shadows, slick and popular guitar bands, seemed out of date. The blues in the hands of Clapton and Mayall seemed so much more mature and to use a phrase increasingly heard – 'heavy'.

The Bluesbreakers album cover quickly became something of a classic in itself, showing Eric sitting calmly reading The Beano, a well known British children's comic, while the rest of the band gazed mournfully into the camera, pondering the meaning of life or their unpaid telephone bills. This little gesture of Eric's – together with his barely concealed grin – showed that his thoughts were always going to be elsewhere, and that he wouldn't be tied down anywhere if he could help it.

But for the moment he gave his all to

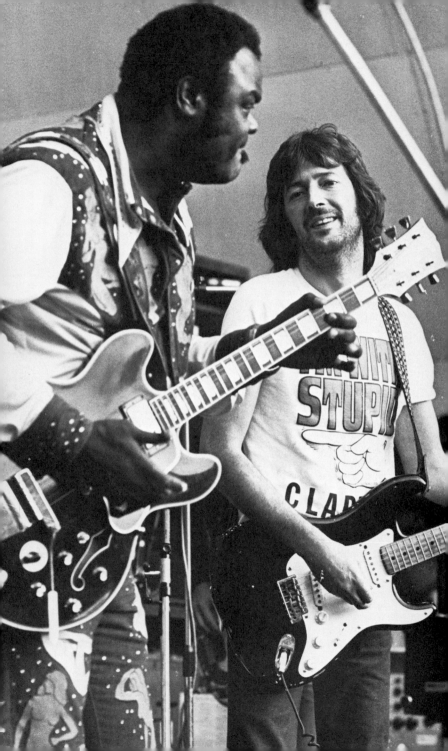

the band, bringing in the crowds while the leader kept an eye on the 'gate'. Eric's guitar sang and expressed ideas in such a lyrical fashion it was not surprising he created an emotional response. There was an almost feminine appeal to the sound. In his hands a guitar was a woman, not a machine, an idea not far removed from B.B. King's concept of his trusty 'Lucille'.

Such cuts as 'All Your Love', 'Hideaway' and 'Steppin' Out' contained some of the finest guitar work of the era: passionate, imaginative and subtle. Not even John Mayall's strangled vocals or Hughie Flint's uneven drumming could detract from the sound of the Clapton guitar in its pristine state. Truly this was an artistic peak never equalled in all the clamour of a thousand guitars since. Such delicate artistic expression could not survive in rock. The pressure was on for Clapton to display himself as a showman, endlessly playing 'Steppin' Out' for audiences hungry for thrills. The lucky ones were those who saw Eric at his peak on those nightly small club gigs during the mid-Sixties. It was often asked in those eager, expectant days how it was young white kids could properly have experienced 'the blues', with their relatively comfortable suburban upbringings. There were blues a plenty ahead.

Apart from the twelve tracks on the Decca 'Bluesbreakers' album Eric was also heard with Mayall on such cuts as 'I'm Your Witch Doctor' and 'Telephone Blues'. Eric also recorded a selection of titles with Jimmy Page and these were later issued together with the John Mayall tracks on 'Blues Anytime Vols. 1 & 2' on Immediate Records. The Clapton-Page collaborations, 'Snake Drive', 'Tribute To Elmore', 'West Coast Idea', 'Draggin' My Tail', 'Freight Loader', and 'Choker' were historically fascinating, though as unaccompanied guitar duets they were not particularly inspired. It was, however, a last opportunity for them to relax and play in unpressured fashion before the maelstrom of the supergroups, Cream and Led Zeppelin, would take over their lives.

Blues producer Mike Vernon and his engineer Gus Dudgeon played a considerable role in ensuring Clapton's talent would be aired in the most sympathetic way.

'Lonely Years', a Mayall-Clapton collaboration featuring vocals, harmonica and guitar, was one of the most deep rooted blues performances of its time. Wrote Mike Vernon on the sleeve notes of the 'Raw Blues' album released on Decca (ACL 1220) in 1967: "Listen to 'Lonely Years' and 'Bernard Jenkins'. Some early style guitar work here . . . never before has such a, dare I say it, authentic sound been created in a British studio. The production was done by Purdah Records, both instruments and voice being recorded on one microphone, hence that weird sound."

Authentic it was. Commercial it wasn't. Indeed it couldn't provide a sufficiently satisfying mode of expression for Clapton. Re-creating the Chicago blues sounds of the Fifties was laudable, but rock music was growing and changing. There were The Beatles and Bob Dylan proving the existence of art in contemporary music. Maybe Eric Clapton could develop and expand, as a writer and singer, as well as a blues guitarist. In the mid-Sixties the sky seemed the limit.

On the blues club and pub scene of the period, with its huge traffic in groups, musicians soon got to know each other, and there was much coveting of different players. While band leaders desperately tried to keep a tight rein on their errant sidemen, the best of them were for ever plotting escape and dangerous liaisons. Eric had replaced Roger Dean in The Bluesbreakers in May 1965 and would leave in June 1966. The band's line-up remained fairly stable during this time with Hughie Flint on drums and John McVie on bass. But on some gigs, there came a fiery Scots bass guitarist who could also sing and play harmonica with an expertise and passion that was awe inspiring. He had served in trad jazz bands before coming south to play with drummer Ginger Baker in The Graham Bond Organisation. This was more of a jazz-blues band. It had achieved huge fan and critical acclaim but was stricken with poverty and problems.

Both Baker and Bruce had great technical skill and drive which far outshone the earnest blues crusaders of the time. Ginger was acclaimed as the man who had defined the future of heavy rock drumming. The only problem was their Scots and Irish temperaments which often clashed during their time with the equally explosive Graham Bond.

Jack Bruce appeared in the Mayall ranks, perhaps seeking sanctuary, and cut a version of 'Stormy Monday Blues' alongside Clapton. This was included in the Decca LP 'John Mayall Looking Back' released in 1969.

When Eric joined Mayall he too had been looking for sanctuary. He said later: "I knew his music and had a soft spot for him and I just made up my mind to join him because I thought it was the only thing to do."

In the event Eric was just as restricted, solo-wise, with The Bluesbreakers on their nightly gig trail as he had been with The Yardbirds. Leaders like to be stars, especially if they play the guitar, keyboards, harmonica and sing. When youthful Jack Bruce arrived and sang the occasional number with real fire, Eric sensed a kindred spirit. "I knew how good he was from then on, he sang a couple of things and they were really great. From then on he was a natural first choice in any group I might dream about forming."

Eric's views on music were changing and he sensed that he couldn't stay recreating Chicago blues forever. He openly admitted "I wanted to go further than the band was going. They were stuck with their thing."

Jack Bruce only served around six weeks with Mayall before joining Manfred Mann, then at the top of the charts with an apparently unstoppable stream of hit singles. "I thought if I joined them I would be rich," said Jack. He was wrong.

Then Ginger Baker, who had been as depressed as Jack about the lack of success enjoyed by the pioneering Bond band, came up with a brilliant idea.

He wanted to form a new group, featuring himself, Jack Bruce and . . . Eric Clapton. They would be the cream of all the musicians on the scene. It was a proud title, but The Cream had softer, sweeter, more palatable connotations as well. The new band would aim for the commercial success that had eluded The Bluesbreakers and The Bond Organisation, but it would still be a musical band, with its roots in the blues that had such a grip on the emotions of young audiences.

Jack and Ginger felt they could bury differences caused by a mutual sense of grievance and frustration. Clapton would be the even-tempered stabilising influence. In fact, it was Eric who came up with the name Cream when the three men played together for the first time in Ginger's front room at his home in Neasden. This early jam had been preceded by a planning meeting the day before at Eric's flat, which transferred to a park, where much cigarette smoke drifted harmlessly in the wind.

I went to see the new band at one of their first rehearsals in a church hall in Putney which was also being used by a troop of Brownies. The giggling eight year olds kindly vacated the premises while Ginger set up his drums and Jack and Eric plugged in. I was thrilled to hear them, and felt very privileged. I had been a particular supporter of all three

musicians in the music press, and Ginger had given me the original story about the group's formation. Indeed when I printed the story three separate managers rang up to deny the existence of the group, representing Manfred Mann, Graham Bond and John Mayall. But Cream were now in the hands of manager Robert Stigwood who took me to one side and asked rather anxiously what I thought of the band. "Were they any good?" I nodded vigorously, somewhat surprised.

The sounds I heard were thrilling. Ginger was playing a kind of marching blues beat rather like Art Blakey. Jack's bass guitar boomed with unnatural power and Eric was wailing with an intensity I'd not heard before.

"They're great," I told Robert. He seemed mightily relieved. After years of bad luck with artists and promotions, he hoped this would be one group to succeed. This they did beyond anyone's wildest expectations. The music echoed around the empty hall with only a stray Brownie and caretaker to hear them. It was very nearly the last time Cream were heard. Jack Bruce volunteered to drive us all back to town in the group's truck, loaded with equipment. We piled into the front seat and Jack pulled straight out into the main road without looking and narrowly avoided an on-coming vehicle. Eric looked askance. Perhaps even then he was wondering if he had done the right thing.

But there was no denying the great excitement engendered by the new band. I saw their first gig in the pouring rain, along with thousands of others at the Windsor Jazz Festival in 1966. The crowd went wild and Cream were a sensation. But underneath their success lay the problem of attitudes and material. There was none available at first. When I saw them rehearsing I think they had three numbers. No modern group of such potential would be so careless. The songs that Eric presented to the band were not suitable and later Jack Bruce emerged as the major songwriter, together with lyricist Pete Brown. They created many of the band's hits like 'Sunshine Of Your Love' and 'Politician'. The former was a million selling single and at last big money rolled in giving the impoverished musicians a taste of big houses, fast cars and high living. The dream nurtured during all the years spent racing up and down the highways in search of gigs, money and fame had come true.

Cream quickly grew out of the small English club circuit. After some memorable concerts at Brian Epstein's

Saville Theatre in London, they went on to achieve huge success in America. They had hit albums too, including 'Fresh Cream', 'Disraeli Gears' and the live double set 'Wheels Of Fire'. Their music was in retrospect a peculiar hybrid of improvisation and songs, but they established the idea of instrumental superiority and laid the foundations for the heavy rock and heavy metal movements.

Cream was destined to have only a short life. Heavy touring took its toll and the musicians came under increasing strain. Eric did not enjoy his role as peace maker and found the others overpowering personalities on and off stage. This wasn't his dream band envisaged in the days with Mayall. Once again I bumped into Eric looking distraught and miserable at what should have been a celebration party for the group at their manager's home. Robert asked me to talk to Eric and try to find out what was wrong. At the time it seemed as if Eric was just looking a gift horse in the mouth. But his instincts and finer feelings were telling him it was time to call a halt.

"I think we began to want to go our own separate ways after the first American tour which lasted four and a half months," revealed Jack Bruce later. "We got tired and turned off Cream and each other." They would have broken up sooner but for the disappointment this would have caused, and resentment too, among those thousands of fans still waiting their chance to see the band everyone was talking about.

Eric's playing on stage began to deteriorate. Gone was the subtle magic of the blues. At one concert at the Saville he suspended his guitar from chains and let it sway about, clanging and feeding back.

But Cream on form were tremendously exciting and the vast majority of audiences thoroughly enjoyed Eric being featured once again on 'Steppin' Out', the fast blues riff, full of breaks in which the guitarist could twist like an eel. The fans didn't know about the pressures on the group wrought by their success and were deeply saddened when Cream announced they would break up. They played their last set at London's Royal Albert Hall on November 26, 1968, and released one more album 'Goodbye' which included 'Badge', a Clapton composition co-written with a new friend George Harrison of The Beatles.

Eric and George had struck up a close friendship. The Beatle greatly admired Clapton's guitar work, and the latter briefly came under Harrison's mystical infuence and took to staring intently at people's eyes and talking about the Lord.

Eric now lived in a fine Surrey mansion with swimming pool, albeit a cracked one with grass growing through. There was an attractive air of faded Thirties splendour about the house and it was here in an upper room that I once had a half-hour jam session with Eric. I played Ginger Baker's drums while Eric played a selection of Buddy Holly hits. A group of stoned hippies sat at our feet. I was in a state of nirvana, and even Eric looked as if he was enjoying himself; I think he appreciated the simple qualities of my drumming after the heavier approach of my predecessor.

The occasion was supposed to be an interview to discuss Eric's next project, a band to be called Blind Faith. This would be another dream band that would go wrong. This time Eric had brought in one of his favourite musicians, Stevie Winwood, once the darling of The Spencer Davis group and then the mainstay of Traffic.

On bass was Rick Grech from Family while Ginger Baker was back again on drums, though it was rumoured that Eric would have preferred to make a clean break from Ginger's style. He was looking for something more laid back and the ideological split was revealed when the band made their debut at a free concert in Hyde Park in June 1969. It was one of those balmy summer days which seemed to characterise the era in the memories of those who lived through them. The actual performance turned out to be something of an anticlimax. Ginger was the only one to try really hard and play in his characteristically driving fashion. But with the weak PA system most of the sound drifted away: Eric spent most of his time leaning against an amplifier looking detached. It turned out that the band had tried some particularly powerful grass just before the gig which rendered them less than dynamic. The music was nice, perfect for a summer's day, but it wasn't the battering riot the ex-Cream fans had come to expect. The album 'Blind Faith' was much better however, and has grown in stature over the years and is now probably more satisfying than many of Cream's more off the wall creations.

Cuts like 'Had To Cry Today' and 'Can't Find My Way Home', by Steve Winwood were very attractive and contained some thoughtful and melodic guitar work. The first of the super groups (as I dubbed them), they had enormous potential, and Eric contributed one of

his finest songs 'Presence Of The Lord' whose lyrics reflected the need of confused young musicians to find some substantial belief in lives assailed by doubts and fears. The piece also showed that Blind Faith could rock out with great violence, and Eric's guitar howled with a vigour that was in a sense a last fling.

The album sold very well but after one troubled tour of America the band broke up, leaving a trail of disappointment and a certain amount of disillusionment amongst British fans in particular who barely had a chance to see the group.

During the 1969 tour Eric met up with another dissatisfied soul, John Lennon, who had set up The Plastic Ono Band. Eric had already established Beatle credentials by playing on the cut 'While My Guitar Gently Weeps' on their famed 'White Album'. Now he sat in with The Plastic Ono Band and appeared on their 'Live Peace In Toronto' album.

While Blind Faith was on the road they were supported by American white soul act Delaney & Bonnie. Eric claimed to like their down home approach in preference to the stale Cream frenzy that surrounded Blind Faith. When the tour finished Eric stayed in New York with them and later brought Delaney & Bonnie to England. They stayed with him at his house, where Bonnie seemed to think she was Lady of the Manor. Many of Eric's friends thought his enthusiasm for the pair was misplaced but they nevertheless appeared on his first solo album 'Eric Clapton' which was cut in Los Angeles and came out in August 1970. Other guests included Leon Russell and Steve Stills. The music had the rough and ready boogie rock quality, typical of the early Seventies feel which permeated the styles of The Rolling Stones, Rod Stewart and The Faces and Joe Cocker. A cut called 'Slunky' typified this approach, messy to British ears and not entirely convincing. Once again on the back liner photograph Eric seemed detached from the band, toying with a species of fruit, heavily bearded, with extra long hair and his eyes averted, while the rest of the crew posed eagerly. They wanted fame. By now Eric was getting sick of it.

On this album Eric showed how much he was developing as a vocalist and he benefited from good engineering on songs like 'Bad Boy'. Delaney Bramlett produced the album at Village Recorders in West Los Angeles and after years of potting shed style British productions, this sounded positively smooth and professional. Bramlett also wrote many of the songs while Eric chose John Cale's 'After Midnight' as another suitable

vehicle. Heavy with arranged brass and white soul backing vocals, it was far removed from the kind of direct interaction between improvising musicians that was the basis of most British rock. As a result U.K. fans listened tight lipped and largely unimpressed. They didn't want to hear a rabble of Americans chanting. Eric's own singing, when it could be heard above the din, was pleasant and relaxed and 'After Midnight' and 'Blues Power' pointed to the style that Eric would pursue for the next decade. He wanted to play songs and lessen the guitar virtuoso image. At first he took this policy to such extremes it was counter-productive and ultimately severely damaging.

Eric went on tour around Europe as a guest with Delaney & Bonnie and also sat in on sessions with George Harrison, Steve Stills, Dr. John and Howlin' Wolf. Then at last he decided to form his own band, but with typical Clapton humour decided to call it Derek and The Dominos. They made their debut at a benefit concert in London in June a month before the release of the 'Eric Clapton' album. The band included Bobby Whitlock, Carl Radle and Jim Gordon, all Americans. At his concerts Eric seemed strangely annoyed and huffy towards his fans, making cutting remarks and ignoring the cries of ex-Cream fans for their favourite numbers.

Bramlett had encouraged Eric to sing more and he now felt sufficiently confident to present himself as the main singer as well as guitarist in his own band. It was a subservient sort of backing group, the kind that professional Americans do so well. They took no risks, kept their noses down (or occasionally up), and sounded for the most part extremely dull. This was apparent on lacklustre performances like 'Tell The Truth' featured on the band's double live album 'Derek & The Dominos In Concert' recorded at the Fillmore East in New York. Eric's talent seemed bogged down in the essential mediocrity of his backing musicians. They could play but they couldn't inspire.

The band's American tour wasn't too successful and the record company had to rush around telling everyone that "Derek Is Eric" to clear up any confusion. In the midst of all this the real Eric had recorded a masterwork that was virtually overlooked. In late 1970 he released the Dominos first studio album 'Layla And Other Assorted Love Songs'. The presence of Duane Allman on guitar helped lift the band and 'Layla' itself, dedicated to George Harrison's wife Patti Boyd, was superb. The song was played

A SHORT BIOGRAPHY

endlessly at London's Speakeasy Club, a well known musicians' haunt, but did not do so well outside. The commercial flop of 'Layla', the subsequent death of Duane Allman in a motor cycle accident in October 1971 coming not long after the death of Jimi Hendrix, one of Eric's idols, in September 1970, all induced a deep depression in Clapton.

On August 1, 1971 Eric played with George Harrison and Bob Dylan at the famed Concert For Bangla Desh, in Madison Square Garden, New York. But Eric's appearances had begun to diminish and his own band eventually broke up. Eric disappeared from view and spent most of his time at his home in Surrey. Friends could only contact him through an elaborate series of coded telephone rings. Then the rumours began to spread that Eric, the most stable of musicians even when surrounded by all kinds of drug users, had succumbed to the use of hard drugs and by all accounts had become a heroin addict. It was a great and needless tragedy, and there was heartfelt concern for him.

It was a source of sadness that a man who had given so much to music should be sitting behind closed doors and wasting away. It seemed there was not much anybody could do when he was so isolated. But efforts were made behind the scenes to bring him back to health and one who made the most strenuous attempts to rebuild his confidence was Pete Townshend of The Who. For two years the healing process went on and then came a call from the Stigwood office to the Melody Maker. "Eric is back." He appeared at a press conference held for him at a Chinese restaurant in London where he sat on the stairs looking dazed and confused, and it seemed, just a shade contrite and guilty.

He made a comeback in front of the public at the Rainbow Theatre in North London. The event was recorded as 'Eric Clapton's Rainbow Concert' (RSO). Eric appeared in a white suit and heavily bearded, accompanied by Pete Townshend and Ronnie Wood on guitars. Behind them were Steve Winwood, Jim Capaldi and Rick Grech.

Among his best albums of the Seventies were 'No Reason To Cry', 'There's One In Every Crowd', 'Backless' and the live set 'E C Was Here'.

The music scene around him changed. Punk rock came along and many of the old idols were overturned and debunked. Clapton's American rock based music did not appeal to the new generation who wanted three minute excitement and revolutionary idealism. Pop music took many new directions

with the advent of electronics, and the re-working of disco disciplines became much more powerful and vibrant. Rock itself was in danger of dying while Heavy Metal, a younger, brasher off-shoot replaced it on the festival and concert circuit.

Clapton retained his respect and audience however, and toured consistently with excellent bands. His health restored and his excessive drinking over, Eric had grown up. He switched from Polydor to Warner Brothers who distributed his best album in years 'Money And Cigarettes' on the Duck label in 1983. This contained another welcome hit single 'I've Got A Rock'n'Roll Heart'. One of my favourite cuts was 'Everybody Oughta Make A Change' which seemed to sum up Eric's life.

The album came in the year that he celebrated twenty years in the music business. Two decades had passed since he joined Casey Jones and the Engineers. It hardly seemed possible. Perhaps spurred by feelings of nostalgia he agreed to appear in a charity concert that year at the Royal Albert Hall in London. It was to raise money for research into a disease that had crippled one of his old friends, Ronnie Lane, once of the Small Faces and The Faces with Rod Stewart.

Eric appeared in a line up with his old sparring partners Jeff Beck and Jimmy Page. Behind them was Stevie Winwood and many other friends. Eric played 'Layla' and its ringing chords and aching melody seemed a hymn for all the years of success, failures, agonies and delights.

With hindsight it would be easy to re-write Eric's life and tell him where he went wrong. He should have recorded a solo album when he was with John Mayall in 1966, or with Stevie Winwood when they were at a peak of their powers. Cream should have spent more time rehearsing and writing and less on hard American touring. Blind Faith should have stayed home to work before going to America. But if he had done all these things perhaps there would have been no 'Layla'. He has had a life time of others trying to direct him. Now he stands alone, free of advice and influences. The man in the smart suit on the cover of 'Money And Cigarettes' is at last looking the camera and – the world – right in the eye.

GROUPS

THE YARDBIRDS

Eric Clapton lead guitar. Chris Dreja rhythm guitar. Keith Relf vocals, harmonica. Paul Samwell-Smith bass. Jim McCarty drums.

Some US copies feature 'I Wish You Could' or 'I'm Not Talking' as B-side.

A-side written by Graham Gouldman, later to find fame in 10cc. This song signalled a more commercial direction which Eric felt was taking them away from their original R&B roots and as a consequence he left the group.

SINGLES

1. I WISH YOU WOULD (Billy Boy Arnold)/A CERTAIN GIRL (Neville)
UK Columbia DB 7283.
US Epic BN9709.
Released July 1964.
Produced by Giorgio Gomelsky.
Recorded at Olympic Studios, London, November 1963.
　　Worth noting that on many of the US labels the title was printed as 'I Which You Could' and that early copies featured 'I Ain't Got You' as B-side.

2. GOOD MORNING LITTLE SCHOOLGIRL (Level, Love)/I AIN'T GOT YOU (Carter)
UK Columbia DB 7391.
No US release.
Released October 1964.
Produced by Giorgio Gomelsky.
Recorded Olympic Studios, London, March 1964.

3. FOR YOUR LOVE (Gouldman)/GOT TO HURRY (Rasoutin)
UK Columbia DB 7499.
US Epic BN 9790.
Released February 1965.
Re-released in UK, August 1976 Charly CS 1012.
Produced by Giorgio Gomelsky.
A-side recorded at IBC Studios, London, December 1964.
B-side recorded at Olympic Studios, London, November 1964.

ALBUMS

1. FIVE LIVE YARDBIRDS
UK Columbia SX1677.
No US release.
Released January 1965.
Produced by Giorgio Gomelsky.
Sound Engineer Philip Wood.
Recorded live at the Marquee Club, London, 1964.
Reissued as 'The Yardbirds Feat. E.C.' August 1977, Charly CR30012.
Reissued as 'Five Live Yardbirds' August 1979, Charly CR 30173.
　　Side One: 1. Too Much Monkey Business (Berry)/2. I Got Love If You Want It (Moore) 3. Smokestack Lightnin' (Burnett)/4. Good Morning Little Schoolgirl (Level, Love)/5. Respectable (Isley Brothers)
　　Side Two: 6. Five Long Years (Boyd)/7. Pretty Girl (Macdaniel)/8. Louise (Hooker)/9. I'm A Man (Pomus, Shuman)10. Here 'Tis (Macdaniel).
　　In Giorgio Gomelsky's words: "Something of the excitement and freshness of the Yardbird sound has been captured on the tape. Some parts of the performance could have been better, maybe the recording itself could be improved on, perhaps? Perhaps, but who knows, it could also have been much worse."

2. SONNY BOY WILLIAMSON AND THE YARDBIRDS
UK Fontana TL5277.
US Mercury SR601071.

Released January 1966.
Philips 6435011. Reissue June 1975.
Recorded at the Crawdaddy Club,
Richmond, October 8, 1963, a club
owned by manager Giorgio Gomelsky.
    Side One: 1. Bye Bye Bird
(Williamson, W. Dixon)/2. Mister
Downchild/3. 23 Hours Too Long/4. Out
Of The Water Coast/5. Baby Don't Worry.*
    Side Two: 6. Pontiac Blues/7. Take It
Easy Baby/8. I Don't Care No More*/
9. Do The Weston.
All songs Williamson except'Bye Bye
Bird.'
*Williamson alone.

3. REMEMBER . . . THE YARDBIRDS
UK Starline SRS5069.
No US release.
Released June 1971.
    A selection of their greatest tracks.
Eric appears only on Smokestack
Lightnin'/I Wish You Would (Alternative
version to single)/Good Morning Little
Schoolgirl/For Your Love/A Certain Girl/
I'm A Man.

RARITIES

1. BOOM BOOM/HONEY IN YOUR HIPS
Holland CBS1433 (Single).
Recorded at R.G. Jones Studios, Surrey,
1963.
    Three tracks were in fact recorded.
The third, 'Baby What's Wrong', can be
found on 'History of British Blues , Vol.1'
(Sire SAS 3701) US.

2. Sonny Boy Williamson/Yardbirds: 'ROCK GENERATION' SERIES, VOL. V
France BYG529 705.
Released July 1972.
Recorded at First Rhythm and Blues
Festival, Birmingham, February 28, 1964.
    Slow Walk/Yardbirds Beat/My Little
Cabin.

THE POWERHOUSE

One off studio band featuring:
Eric Clapton guitar. Jack Bruce bass.
Paul Jones vocals. Stevie Winwood
keyboards. Pete Yorn drums.

ALBUMS

1. WHAT'S SHAKIN'
Elektra EKS 7304.
Released June 1966.
    I Want To Know (S. Macleod)/
Crossroads (R. Johnson)/Steppin' Out (M.
Slim).

JOHN MAYALL'S BLUESBREAKERS

John Mayall vocals, piano, organ,
harmonica. Eric Clapton vocals, guitar.
John McVie bass. Hughie Flint drums.

SINGLES

1. I'M YOUR WITCH DOCTOR (Mayall)/TELEPHONE BLUES (Mayall)
UK Immediate IM 012.
Released October 1965.
Produced by Jimmy Page.
Recorded during Eric's first stint with
John Mayall. He'd left JM for a pick-up

band to tour Greece. This lasted only a few months and he returned to the relief of Mayall who realised Eric's potential.

2. LONELY YEARS (Mayall)/ BERNARD JENKINS (Clapton)
UK Purdah 3502.
Released August 1966.
Produced by Mike Vernon.
Recorded at Wessex Studios, London.
    Original pressing of 500.

3. PARCHMENT FARM (Allison)/ KEY TO LOVE (Mayall)
UK Decca F12490.
Released September 1966.
    Both tracks can be found on the Bluesbreakers LP.

2. RAW BLUES
UK Ace of Clubs SLC 1220.
US London PS543.
Released January 1967.
    Various artists compilation on which 'Bernard Jenkins' and 'Lonely Years' can be found.

CREAM

Eric Clapton guitar, vocals. Jack Bruce bass, vocals. Ginger Baker drums.

ALBUMS

GROUPS

1. BLUESBREAKERS WITH ERIC CLAPTON
UK Decca SKL4804.
US London PS 492.
Released July 1966.
Produced by Mike Vernon.
Engineer Gus Dudgeon.
Recorded at Decca Studios, London, in Studio 2.
    Side One: 1. All Your Love (Ruch, Dixon)/2. Hideway (King, Thompson)/ 3. Little Girl (Mayall)/4. Another Man (Arr. Mayall)/5. Double Crossing Time (Mayall, Clapton)/6. What'd I Say (Charles).
    Side Two: 7. Key To Love (Mayall)/ 8. Parchment Farm (Allison)/9. Have You Heard (Mayall)/10. Ramblin' On My Mind (Johnson)/11. Steppin' Out (L.C.Frazier)/ 12. It Ain't Right (Jacobs).

SINGLES

1. WRAPPING PAPER (Bruce, Brown)/CAT'S SQUIRREL (Trad. Arr. S. Splurge)
UK Reaction 591007.
Released October 1966.
    Strange release as first single for a new supergroup, with little musical content and no guitar to speak of. It sold poorly as a consequence, not even making the top twenty.

2. I FEEL FREE (Bruce, Brown)/ N.S.U. (Bruce)
UK Reaction 591011.
Released December 1966.
    A much better choice after a disappointing first release. 'I Feel Free' also featured the then revolutionary 'Woman Tone' which Eric obtained by cutting out the bass and turning up full the treble and volume controls on his guitar.

3. STRANGE BREW (Clapton, Collins, Pappalardi)/TALES OF BRAVE ULYSSES (Clapton, Sharp)
UK Reaction 591015.
Released June 1967.

4. ANYONE FOR TENNIS (Clapton, Sharp)/PRESSED RAT AND WARTHOG (Baker)
UK Polydor 56258.
Released May 1968.
    A-side is theme from 'Savage Seven' film.

5. SUNSHINE OF YOUR LOVE (Bruce, Brown, Clapton)/SWLABR (Bruce, Brown)
UK Polydor 56286.
US Atco 6544.
Released September 1968.

6. WHITE ROOM (Bruce, Brown)/ THOSE WERE THE DAYS (Baker, Taylor)
UK Polydor 56300.
US Atco 6617.
Released January 1969.

7. BADGE (Clapton, George Harrison)/WHAT A BRINGDOWN (Ginger Baker)
UK Polydor 56315.
Released April 1969.
George Harrison co-wrote 'Badge' and also played rhythm guitar on this track under the name of L'Angelo Misterioso. Clapton later returned the compliment and played on George's 'While My Guitar Gently Weeps' on The Beatles' 'White Album'.

8. I FEEL FREE (Bruce, Brown)/ WRAPPING PAPER (Bruce, Brown)
UK reissue Polydor 2056120.
Released July 1971.

9. BADGE (Clapton, Harrison)/ WHAT A BRINGDOWN (Baker)
UK reissue Polydor 2058285.
Released October 1972.

ALBUMS

1. FRESH CREAM
UK Reaction 593001 Mono. Reaction 594001 Stereo.
US Atco SD 33-206.
Released December 1966.
Produced by Robert Stigwood.
Side One: 1. N.S.U. (Bruce)/2. Sleepy Time (Godfrey, Bruce)/3. Dreaming (Bruce)/4. Sweet Wine (Godfrey, Baker)/ 5. Spoonful (Willie Dixon).
Side Two: 6. Cat's Squirrel (Trad. Arr. S. Splurge)/7. Four Until Late (Robert Johnson)/8. Rollin' And Tumblin' (Muddy Waters)/9. I'm So Glad (Skip James)/ 10. Toad (Baker).
Reissued as 'Full Cream', October 1970, UK Polydor 2447010.
Reissued as 'Cream', March 1975, UK Polydor 2384067. Includes two extra tracks: 'Wrapping Paper' and 'Coffee Song'.
Reissued 1978, US RSO 13009.

GROUPS

2. DISRAELI GEARS
UK Reaction 593003 Mono. Reaction 593003 Stereo.
US Atco 33-232.
Released November 1967.
Reissued January 1978, UK RSO 2394129.
Reissued 1978, US RSO 13010.
Produced by Felix Pappalardi.
Recorded at Atlantic Studios, New York.
Side One: 1. Strange Brew (Clapton, Collins, Pappalardi)/2. Sunshine Of Your Love (Bruce, Brown, Clapton)/3. World Of Pain (Collins, Pappalardi)/4. Dance The Night Away (Bruce, Brown)/5. Blue Condition (Baker).
Side Two: 6. Tales Of Brave Ulysses (Clapton, Sharp)/7. Swlabr (Bruce, Brown)/8. We're Going Wrong (Bruce)/ 9. Outside Woman Blues (Reynolds, Arr. Clapton)/10. Take It Back (Bruce, Brown)/ 11. Mother's Lament (Trad. Arr. Cream).

Side One: 1. I'm So Glad (Skip James)/2. Politician (Bruce, Brown).
Side Two: 3. Sitting On Top Of The World (Burnett)/4. Badge (Clapton, Harrison)/5. Doing That Scrapyard Thing (Bruce, Brown) 6. What A Bringdown (Baker).

3. WHEELS OF FIRE (Double)
UK Polydor 583031/2 Mono. 583031/2 Stereo.
US Atco SD 2-700.
Released August 1968.
In the studio: UK Polydor 582033 Mono. 583033 Stereo. Released August 1968.
UK RSO 2671109. Reissue January 1978.
US RSO 23802. Reissue 1978.
UK RSO 2394136. Reissue January 1978.
Live At The Fillmore: UK Polydor 582040 Mono. 583040 Stereo. Released December 1968.
UK RSO 2394137. Reissue January 1978.
Produced by Felix Pappalardi.
Studio album recorded at Atlantic Recording Studios, New York.
Live album recorded at Fillmore West, San Francisco.
Side One: 1. White Room (Bruce, Baker)/2. Sitting On Top Of The World (Burnett)/3. Passing The Time (Baker, Taylor)/4. As You Said (Bruce, Brown).
Side Two: 5. Pressed Rat And Warthog (Baker, Taylor)/6. Politician (Bruce, Brown)/7. Those Were The Days (Baker, Taylor)/8. Born Under A Bad Sign (Jones, Bell)/9. Deserted Cities Of The Heart (Bruce, Brown).
Side Three: 10. Crossroads (Robert Johnson)/11. Spoonful (Willie Dixon).
Side Four: 12. Traintime (Jack Bruce)/ 13. Toad (Ginger Baker).

4. GOODBYE
UK Polydor 583053.
US Atco SD7001.
Released March 1969.
UK RSO 2394178. Reissue January 1978.
Produced by Felix Pappalardi.

5. LIVE CREAM, VOL. 1
UK Polydor 2383 016.
US Atco 33328.
Released June 1970.
UK RSO 2394154.
US RSO 13014.
Reissue January 1978.
Produced by Felix Pappalardi.
'Lawdy Mama' produced by Ahmet Ertegun and Robert Stigwood.
Side One: 1. N.S.U. (Bruce)/2. Sleepy Time Time (Bruce, Godfrey)/3. Lawdy Mama (Trad. Arr. Clapton).
Side Two: 4. Sweet Wine (Baker, Godfrey)/5. Rollin' And Tumblin' (Waters).

6. LIVE CREAM, VOL. 2
UK Polydor 2383 119.
US Atco SD 7005.
Released July 1972.
UK RSO 2394155.
US RSO 13015.
Reissue January 1978.
Produced by Felix Pappalardi.
   Side One: 1. Deserted Cities Of The Heart (Bruce, Brown)/2. White Room (Bruce, Brown)/3. Politician (Bruce, Brown)/4. Tales Of Brave Ulysses (Clapton, Sharp).
   Side Two: 5. Sunshine Of Your Love (Bruce, Brown)/6. Hideaway (King, Thompson).

SINGLES

1. ISLAND PROMO SINGLE (Double A-side)
   Instrumental jam.
   Issued by Island in pressing of 500 to notify change of address.

ALBUMS

1. BLIND FAITH
UK Polydor 583059.
US Atco SD 33-304.
Released August 1969.
Produced by Jimmy Miller.
RSO 2394 142. Reissue 1977.
   Side One: 1. Had To Cry Today (Winwood)/2. Can't Find My Way Home (Winwood)/3. Well All Right (Petty, Holly, Allison, Mauldin)/4. Presence Of The Lord (Clapton).
   Side Two: 5. Sea Of Joy (Winwood)/ 6. Do What You Like (Baker).

GROUPS

BLIND FAITH

Eric Clapton guitar, vocals. Stevie Winwood keyboards, vocals. Rick Grech bass. Ginger Baker drums.

DELANEY AND BONNIE

SINGLES

1. COMIN' HOME (B.Bramlett, Clapton)/GROUPIE (SUPERSTAR) (B.Bramlett, Russell)
Atlantic 584 308.
Released 1969.

ALBUMS

GROUPS

Ford and D. Bramlett, Russell)/3. Only You Know And I Know (D. Mason)/4. I Don't Want To Discuss It (Beatty, Cooper, Shelby).
   Side Two: 5. That's What My Man Is For (Bessie Griffin)/6. Where There's A Will, There's A Way (B. Bramlett, Whitlock)/7. Coming Home (B. Bramlett, Clapton)/8. Little Richard Medley – Long Tall Sally (Penniman, Blackwell)/Jenny Jenny (Penniman)/The Girl Can't Help It (Trout)/Tutti Frutti (Penniman).

2. DELANEY AND BONNIE – TOGETHER
CBS 64959.
Released 1972.
Produced by Delaney Bramlett.
   Eric plays on 'Comin' Home'/'Groupie (Superstar)'.

1. ON TOUR
UK Atlantic 2400013.
US Atco SD 33-326.
Released 1970.
Produced by Jimmy Miller and Delaney Bramlett.
   Side One: 1. Things Get Better (Floyd, Cropper, Wayne)/2. Poor Elijah – Tribute To Elmore Johnson (Medley) (D. Bramlett,

PLASTIC ONO BAND

John Lennon guitar, vocals. Yoko Ono vocals. Alan White drums.
Klaus Voorman bass. Eric Clapton guitar.

SINGLES

Alan White drums. Jim Gordon drums. Billy Preston organ. Nicky Hopkins piano.

1. COLD TURKEY (Lennon)/DON'T WORRY KYOKO (Yoko Ono)
UK Apple 1001 USA 1813.
Released October 1969.
Produced by John and Yoko.

2. INSTANT KARMA (Lennon)/WHO HAS SEEN THE WIND (Yoko Ono)
UK Apple 1003.
Released February 1970.
Produced by John and Yoko.
   Apple employee Bill Oakes in Rolling Stone, January 22, 1981 issue: "That afternoon, he (John Lennon) sat down at the piano and began banging out 'Instant Karma' then he had me round up a bunch of guys like Alan White and Eric Clapton, and they went into the studio that night."
   B-Side does not feature Clapton.

ALBUMS

1. LIVE PEACE IN TORONTO 1969
UK Apple Core 2001
USA SW3362.
Released December 1969.
Produced by John and Yoko.
Recorded at Toronto Rock 'n' Roll Revival Festival, September 13, 1969.
   Side One: 1. Blue Suede Shoes (Perkins)/2. Money (Bradford, Gordy)/3. Dizzy Miss Lizzy (Williams)/4. Yer Blues (Lennon, McCartney)/5. Cold Turkey (Lennon)/6. Give Peace A Chance (Lennon, McCartney).
   Side Two: 7. Don't Worry Kyoko (Mummy's Only Looking For Her Hand In The Snow) (Yoko Ono)/8. John John (Let's Hope For Peace) (Yoko Ono).

2. SOMETIME IN NEW YORK CITY
UK Apple PCSP716.
USA SVBB3392.
Released September 1972.
Live side recorded at the Lyceum, London, December 15, 1969.
   Tracks: Cold Turkey (Lennon)/Don't Worry Kyoko (Yoko Ono).
   George Harrison guitar. Klaus Voorman bass. Eric Clapton guitar. John Lennon guitar, vocals. Delaney and Bonnie guitar, vocals. Keith Moon drums.

GROUPS

Atlantic
has nothing to say...

except

DELANEY & BONNIE
& FRIENDS
ON TOUR
WITH ERIC CLAPTON

or maybe

LED ZEPPELIN?..... CROSBY, STILLS, NASH & YOUNG?..... LORD SUTCH?
'Led Zeppelin 2'   'Déjà Vu'   '& Heavy Friends'

COMPILATIONS AND ANTHOLOGIES

1. RAW BLUES
Ace of Clubs SLC1220.
Released 1967.

2. BEST OF CREAM
Polydor 583060.
Released 1969.

3. LOOKING BACK
John Mayall.
Decca SKL 5010.
Released 1970.

4. THE WORLD OF JOHN MAYALL, Vol. 1
Decca SPA47.
Released 1970.

5. THE WORLD OF JOHN MAYALL, Vol. 2
Decca SPA138.
Released 1971.

6. THROUGH THE YEARS
John Mayall.
Decca SKL 5086.
Released 1971.

7. REMEMBER THE YARDBIRDS
Starline SRS 5069.
Released 1971.

8. THE HISTORY OF ERIC CLAPTON
Polydor 2659 012.
Released 1972.

9. ERIC CLAPTON AT HIS BEST
RSO 2659 025.
Released 1972.

10. THE BEST OF DELANEY AND BONNIE
Atlantic K40429.
Released 1973.

11. HEAVY CREAM
Polydor 2659022.
Released 1973.

12. THE BLUES WORLD OF ERIC CLAPTON
Decca SPA 387.
Released 1975.

13. BACKTRACKIN'
Eric 1.
Released June 1984.

1st

CREAM

recording

WRAPPING PAPER

reaction

591 007

ERIC CLAPTON - SOLO

SINGLES

**1. AFTER MIDNIGHT (J.J.Cale)/
EASY NOW (Clapton)**
UK Polydor 2001 096.
Released October 1970.

ALBUMS

1. ERIC CLAPTON
UK Polydor 2383021.
US Atco SD33329.
Released August 1970.
Produced by Delaney Bramlett.
Recorded at Village Recorders, West
Los Angeles.
    Side One: 1. Slunky (Bramlett,
Clapton)/2. Bad Boy (Bramlett, Clapton)/
3. Told You For The Last Time (Bramlett,
Cropper)/4. After Midnight (J.J.Cale)/
5. Easy Now (Clapton)/6. Blues Power
(Clapton, Russell).
    Side Two: 7. Bottle Of Red Wine
(Bramlett, Clapton)/8. Lovin' You Lovin'
Me (Bramlett, Clapton)/9. Lonesome And
A Long Way From Home (Bramlett,
Russell)/10. Don't Know Why (Bramlett,
Clapton)/11. Let It Rain (Bramlett,
Clapton).
    The first test pressing of this LP is
different from the product that was finally
released in as much as it contains more
guitar solos and is an alternate mix.

27

DEREK AND THE DOMINOS

Eric Clapton guitar, vocals. Jim Gordon drums. Carl Radle bass. Bobby Whitlock keyboards, vocals.

SINGLES

ERIC CLAPTON · SOLO

1. TELL THE TRUTH (Clapton, Whitlock)/ROLL IT OVER (Clapton, Bramlett)

UK Polydor 2058057.
US Atco 456780.
Released September 1970.
Produced by Phil Spector.
    This single was withdrawn only a few days after release due to Clapton's dissatisfaction with his new band's first release. The Spector produced version of 'Tell The Truth' can now be found only on 'History Of Eric Clapton' (Double LP). 'Roll It Over' is not available.

2. LAYLA (Clapton, Gordon)/BELL BOTTOM BLUES (Clapton)

UK Polydor 2058130.
US Atco 6809.
Released November 1970.
Reissued July 1972.
Produced by Tom Dowd and The Dominos.
Recorded at Criteria Studios, Miami.
    When first released 'Layla' did very little, probably due to Eric's deliberate low profile, much to the chagrin of all concerned. However it became a huge hit when reissued in July 1972.

ALBUMS

1. LAYLA AND OTHER ASSORTED LOVE SONGS (Double)

UK Polydor 2625005.
US Atco SD 2704.
Released December 1970.
Produced by Tom Dowd and The Dominos.

Recorded at Criteria Studios, Miami.
    Side One: 1. I Looked Away (Clapton, Whitlock)/2. Bell Bottom Blues (Clapton)/3. Keep On Growing (Clapton, Whitlock)/4. Nobody Loves You When You're Down And Out (Cox).
    Side Two: 5. I Am Yours (Clapton, Nizami)/6. Anyday (Clapton, Whitlock)/7. Key To The Highway (Segar, Broonzy).
    Side Three: 8. Tell The Truth (Clapton, Whitlock)/9. Why Does Love Got To Be So Sad? (Clapton, Whitlock)/10. Have You Ever Loved A Woman? (Myles).
    Side Four: 11. Little Wing (Hendrix)/12. It's Too Late (Willis)/13. Layla (Clapton, Gordon)/14. Thorn Tree In The Garden (Whitlock).

2. IN CONCERT (Double)

UK RSO 2659020.
US RSO 502-8800.
Released March 1973.
Engineer Eddie Kramer.
Recorded at the Fillmore East, New York, November 1970.
    Side One: 1. Why Does Love Got To Be So Sad? (Clapton, Whitlock)/2. Got To Get Better In A Little While (Clapton).
    Side Two: 3. Let It Rain (Clapton, Bramlett)/4. Presence Of The Lord (Clapton).
    Side Three: 5. Tell The Truth (Clapton, Whitlock)/6. Bottle Of Red Wine (Clapton, Bramlett).
    Side Four: 7. Roll It Over (Clapton, Bramlett)/8. Blues Power (Clapton, Russell)/9. Have You Ever Loved A Woman? (Myles).

THE SILENT YEARS

After the commercial failure of 'Layla' and various other reasons which have already been well publicised elsewhere, Eric disappeared from the music scene for almost two years, making only brief appearances with George Harrison at the Bangla Desh concert in 1971 and with Leon Russell at the Rainbow in the same year.

To make up for lack of new material, Polydor released a fine double album tracing Eric's career from The Yardbirds through to Derek and The Dominos, including an unreleased jam and various session items.

ALBUMS

1. HISTORY OF ERIC CLAPTON (Double)
UK Polydor 2659012.
US Atco SD 2-803.
Released July 1972.

Side One: 1. I Ain't Got You (Carter)/ 2. Hideaway (King)/3. Tribute To Elmore (Clapton, Page)/4. I Want To Know (Macleod)/5. Sunshine Of Your Love (Bruce, Brown, Clapton)/6. Crossroads (Johnson).

Side Two: 7. Sea Of Joy (Winwood)/ 8. Only You Know And I Know (Mason)/ 9. I Don't Want To Discuss It (Beatty, Cooper, Shelby)/10. Teasin' (Ousley)/ 11. Blues Power (Clapton, Russell).

Side Three: 12. Spoonful (Dixon)/ 13. Badge (Clapton, Harrison).

Side Four: 14. Tell The Truth (Clapton, Whitlock)/15. Tell The Truth (Clapton, Whitlock) jam/16. Layla (Clapton, Gordon).

HISTORY OF ERIC CLAPTON

THE COMEBACK
ALBUMS

1. RAINBOW CONCERT
UK RSO 2394116.
US RSO 50877.
Released September 1973.
Produced by Bob Pridden.
Recorded at the Rainbow Theatre,
January 13, 1973, from 6.30 and 8.30
shows.

His back-up band for this one-off
occasion: Ronnie Wood guitar, vocals.
Pete Townshend guitar, vocals. Rick
Grech bass. Steve Winwood keyboards,
vocals. Jim Capaldi drums. Jimmy
Karstein drums. Rebop percussion.

Side One: 1. Badge (Clapton,
Harrison)/2. Roll It Over (Clapton,
Whitlock)/3. Presence Of The Lord
(Clapton).

Side Two: 4. Pearly Queen (Winwood,
Capaldi)/5. After Midnight (Cale)/6. Little
Wing (Hendrix).

Eric Clapton's new album.

ERIC CLAPTON AND HIS BAND

SINGLES

1. I SHOT THE SHERIFF (Marley)/ GIVE ME STRENGTH (Clapton)
UK RSO 2090132.
US RSO 409.
Released July 1974.
Both tracks can be found on the LP '461 Ocean Boulevard'.

2. WILLIE AND THE HAND JIVE (Johnny Otis)/MAINLINE FLORIDA (George Terry)
UK RSO 2090139.
US RSO 503.
Released October 1974.
Both tracks can be found on the LP '461 Ocean Boulevard'.

3. SWING LOW SWEET CHARIOT (Trad. Arr. Clapton)/PRETTY BLUE EYES (Clapton)
UK RSO 2090 158.

Released May 1975.
Both tracks can be found on the LP 'There's One In Every Crowd'.

4. KNOCKING ON HEAVEN'S DOOR (Dylan)/SOMEONE LIKE YOU (Louis)
UK RSO 2090 166.
Released August 1975.

5. HELLO OLD FRIEND (Clapton)/ ALL OUR PASTIMES (Clapton, Danko)
UK RSO 2090 208.
US RSO 861.
Released October 1976.
Both tracks can be found on the LP 'No Reason To Cry'.

6. CARNIVAL (Clapton)/HUNGRY (Sims, Levy)
UK RSO 2090 222.
Released February 1977.
Both tracks can be found on the LP 'No Reason To Cry'.

7. LAY DOWN SALLY (Levy, Clapton)/COCAINE (Cale)
UK RSO 2090 264.

US RSO 886.
Released November 1977.
　Both tracks can be found on the LP 'Slowhand'.

8. WONDERFUL TONIGHT (Clapton)/PEACHES AND DIESEL (Galuten, Clapton)
UK RSO 2090 275.
US RSO 895.
Released March 1978.
　Both tracks can be found on the LP 'Slowhand'. B-side's title was inspired by the group No Dice who were recording in the studio next to Eric.

9. PROMISES (Feldman, Linn)/WATCH OUT FOR LUCY (Clapton)
UK RSO 21.
US RSO 910.
Released October 1978.
　Both tracks can be found on the LP 'Slowhand'.

10. IF I DON'T BE THERE BY MORNING (Dylan)/TULSA TIME (Flowers)
UK RSO 24.
Released March 1979.
　Both tracks can be found on the LP 'Backless'.
　A-side is an otherwise unreleased Bob Dylan song.
　B-side is written by Don William's scratch band guitarist Danny Flowers.
　Clapton had struck up a close relationship with Don Williams and both admired each other's music. Clapton in fact played with him at Hammersmith Odeon in 1978.

11. I CAN'T STAND IT (Clapton)/BLACK ROSE (Troy Seals, Eddie Setser)
UK RSO 74.
US RSO 1060.

Released February 1981.
　Both tracks can be found on the LP 'Another Ticket'.

12. ANOTHER TICKET (Clapton)/RITA MAE (Clapton)
UK RSO 75.
Released April 1981.
　Both tracks can be found on the LP 'Another Ticket'.

13. LAYLA (Clapton, Gordon)/WONDERFUL TONIGHT (Clapton)
UK RSO 87 (7"). RSOX 87 (12").
Released February 1982.
　A-side comes from the LP 'Time Pieces – The Best Of Eric Clapton'.
　B-side is a live version from the LP 'Just One Night'.
　Eric's contract with RSO had expired so they decided to milk their back catalogue in the form of Greatest Hits.

ERIC CLAPTON AND HIS BAND

address at which advance ticket details for his upcoming UK tour could be obtained.

14. I SHOT THE SHERIFF (Marley) COCAINE (Cale)
UK RSO 88 (7″). RSOX (12″).
Released May 1982.
12″ contains a bonus track of 'Knockin' On Heaven's Door'. A previously unavailable live version from the Budokan, December 1979.

15. I'VE GOT A ROCK AND ROLL HEART (Seals, Setser, Diamond)/ MAN IN LOVE (Clapton)
UK W9780 (7″). W9780T (12″).
Released 1983.
Both tracks can be found on the LP 'Money and Cigarettes'.
12″ contains bonus track of 'Everybody Oughta Make A Change'.
Eric's first release on his own label, Duck Records, which also included an

16. THE SHAPE YOU'RE IN (Clapton)/CROSSCUT SAW (Ford)
UK W9701 (7″). W9701T (12″).
Released 1983.
Both tracks can be found on the LP 'Money and Cigarettes'.
12″ contains bonus track of 'Pretty Girl'.

17. SLOW DOWN LINDA (Clapton)/ CRAZY COUNTRY HOP (J. Otis)
UK W9651.
Released 1983.
Both tracks can be found on the LP 'Money and Cigarettes'.
A 12″ release had been planned with a bonus live version of 'The Shape You're In' but this was never released.

ERIC CLAPTON AND HIS BAND

ALBUMS

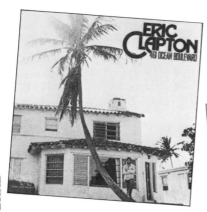

1. 461 OCEAN BOULEVARD
UK RSO 2479 118.
US RSO SO 4801.
Released August 1974.
Produced by Tom Dowd.
Recorded at Criteria Studios, Miami.
Side One: Motherless Children (Trad. Arr. Eric Clapton)/2. Give Me Strength (Clapton)/3. Willie And The Hand Jive (Otis)/4. Get Ready (Clapton, Elliman)/5. I Shot The Sheriff (Marley).

Side Two: 6. I Can't Hold Out Much Longer (James)/7. Please Be With Me (Scot-Boyer)/8. Let It Grow (Clapton)/9. Steady Rollin' May (Johnson)/10. Mainline Florida (Terry).

Eric Clapton guitar, vocals. George Terry guitar. Dick Sims keyboards. Carl Radle bass. Jamie Oldaker drums. Albuy Galuten keyboards. Yvonne Elliman vocals.

Al Jackson of Booker T and The MG's plays drums on Side One Track 2.

This was Eric's comeback album after his lengthy retirement and was well received despite the deliberate lack of guitar solos.

2. THERE'S ONE IN EVERY CROWD
UK RSO 2479132.
US RSO SO 4806.
Released April 1975.
Produced by Tom Dowd.
Recorded at Dynamic Sounds Studio, Kingston, Jamaica and Criteria Studios, Miami.
Side One: 1. We've Been Told (Jesus Coming Soon) (Johnson, Arr. by Clapton)/2. Swing Low Sweet Chariot (Trad. Arr. by Clapton)/3. Little Rachel (Byfield)/4. Don't Blame Me (Clapton, Terry)/5. The Sky Is Crying (James, Robinson).

Side Two: 6. Singin' The Blues (McCreary)/7. Better Make It Through Today (Clapton)/8. Pretty Blue Eyes (Clapton)/9. High (Clapton)/10. Opposites (Clapton).

Personnel same as '461 Ocean Boulevard' with the addition of Marcy Levy vocals.

First pressings of this LP included a drawing by Eric Clapton on the insert.

3. EC WAS HERE
UK RSO 2394160.
US RSO SO 4809.
Released August 1975.
Produced by Tom Dowd.
Side One: 1. Have You Ever Loved A Woman? (Myles)/2. Presence Of The Lord (Clapton)/3. Drifting Blues (Moore, Brown, Williams).

Side Two: 4. Can't Find My Way Home (Winwood)/5. Rambling On My Mind (Trad. Arr. by Clapton)/6. Further On Up The Road (Veasey, Robey).

Track 1 Side One and Track 1 Side Two recorded at Long Beach Arena, July 19, 1974.

Tracks 2 and 3 Side One recorded at Long Beach Arena, July 20, 1974.

Track 2 Side Two recorded at Hammersmith Odeon, London, December 4, 1974.

Track 3 Side Two recorded during the early part of the 1975 tour of North America.

'Ramblin' On My Mind' from Hammersmith Odeon has been cut as the fabulous version of 'Have You Ever Loved A Woman?' in the middle section is no longer there.

USA shows recorded on Wally Heider

Mobile Unit and Record Plant Mobile Unit.

Hammersmith Odeon show recorded on Ronnie Lane's Mobile Unit.

Personnel is same as 'There's One In Every Crowd'.

Personnel is same as previous LP with addition of Sergio Pastora Rodriguez percussion, who joined the band half way through the 1975 USA tour and stayed with them till 1977.

There were several famous guests on the LP including Ron Wood, Bob Dylan, The Band, Georgie Fame.

4. NO REASON TO CRY
UK RSO 2394160.
US RSO 1-3004.
Released August 1976.
Produced by Rob Fraboni.
Recorded at Shangri La Studios and The Village Recorder, New York.

Side One: 1. Beautiful Thing (Manuel, Danko)/2. Carnival (Clapton)/3. Sign Language (Dylan)/4. County Jail Blues (Fields)/5. All Our Past Times (Clapton, Danko).

Side Two: 6. Hello Old Friend (Clapton)/7. Double Trouble (Rush)/ 8. Innocent Times (Clapton, Levy)/ 9. Hungry (Sims, Levy)/10. Black Summer (Clapton).

5. SLOWHAND
UK RSO 2479201.
US RSO RS 1-3030.
Released November 1977.
Produced by Glyn Johns.
Recorded at Olympic Studios, London.

Side One: 1. Cocaine (Cale)/ 2. Wonderful Tonight (Clapton)/3. Lay Down Sally (Levy, Clapton)/4. We're All The Way (Williams).

Side Two: 5. The Core (Levy, Clapton)/ 6. May You Never (Martyn)/7. Mean Old Frisco (Trad.)/8. Peaches and Diesel (Galuten, Clapton).

Personnel is same as previous LP less Sergio Pastora but with the addition of Mel Collins saxophone.

6. BACKLESS
UK RSO 5001.
US RSO RS 1-3039.
Released November 1978.
Produced by Glyn Johns.
Recorded at Olympic Studios, London.

Side One: 1. Walk Out In The Rain (Dylan)/2. Watch Out For Lucy (Clapton)/ 3. I'll Make Love To You (Cale)/4. Roll It (Levy, Clapton)/5. Tell Me That You Love Me (Clapton).

Side Two: 6. If I Don't Be There By Morning (Dylan)/7. Early In The Morning (Arr. Clapton)/8. Promises (Feldman, Linn)/9. Golden Ring (Clapton)/10. Tulsa Time (Flowers).

Personnel is same as previous LP

ERIC CLAPTON AND HIS BAND

minus Yvonne Elliman who had now gone solo.

This was also the last LP with The American Band.

7. JUST ONE NIGHT (Double)
UK RSDX 2.
US RSO RS 2-4202.
Released May 1980.
Produced by Jon Astley.
Recorded at the Budokan in Tokyo, Japan, December 1979.

Side One: 1. Tulsa Time (Flowers)/
2. Early In The Morning (Arr. Clapton)/
3. Lay Down Sally (Levy, Clapton)/
4. Wonderful Tonight (Clapton).

Side Two: 5. If I Don't Be There By Morning (Dylan)/6. Worried Life Blues (Merriweather)/7. All Our Past Times (Clapton, Danko)/8. After Midnight (Cale).

Side Three: 9. Double Trouble (Rush)/
10. Setting Me Up (Knopfler)/11. Blues Power (Clapton/Russell),

Side Four: 12. Rambling On My Mind

(Trad. Arr. Clapton)/13. Cocaine (Cale)/14. Further On Up The Road (Veasey, Robey).

First record to feature the new all British Eric Clapton Band: Henry Spinetti drums. Chris Stainton keyboards. Albert Lee guitar, keyboards, vocals. Dave Markee bass.

8. ANOTHER TICKET
UK RSO 5008.
US RSO RX 1-3095.
Released February 1981.
Produced by Tom Dowd.
Recorded at Compass Point Studios, Nassau, Bahamas.

Side One: 1. Something Special (Clapton)/2. Black Rose (Seals, Setser)/
3. Blow Wind Blow (Morganfield)/
4. Another Ticket (Clapton)/5. I Can't Stand It (Clapton).

Side Two: 6. Hold Me Lord (Clapton)/
7. Floating Bridge (Sleepy John Estes)/
8. Catch Me If You Can (Clapton, Brooker)/9. Rita Mae (Clapton).

Personnel is same as previous LP with the addition of Gary Brooker on keyboards and vocals.

9. MONEY AND CIGARETTES
UK W 3773.
Released February 1983.
Produced by Tom Dowd.
Recorded at Compass Point Studios, Nassau, Bahamas.

Side One: 1. Everybody Oughta Make A Change (Sleepy John Estes)/
2. The Shape You're In (Clapton)/
3. Ain't Going Down (Clapton)/4. I've Got A Rock 'n' Roll Heart (Seals, Setser, Diamond)/5. Man Overboard (Clapton).

Side Two: 6. Pretty Girl (Clapton)/
7. Man In Love (Clapton)/8. Crosscut Saw (Ford)/9. Slow Down Linda (Clapton)/
10. Crazy Country Hop (Otis).

Brand new band featuring:
Donald 'Duck' Dunn bass who used to play in Booker T and The MG's. Roger Hawkins drums. Albert Lee keyboards, vocals, guitars. Special guest on this LP was Ry Cooder slide and electric guitars.

Since making this LP Roger Hawkins has been replaced by the original EC Band drummer Jamie Oldaker.

COMPILATIONS

1. TIME PIECES, VOL. 1
RSO RSD 5010.
Released 1982.
I Shot The Sheriff/After Midnight/ Knockin' On Heaven's Door/Wonderful Tonight/Layla/Cocaine/Lay Down Sally/ Willie And The Hand Jive/Promises/ Swing Low Sweet Chariot/Let It Grow.

2. TIME PIECES, VOL. 2
Live recordings in the Seventies.
RSO RSD 5022.
Released May 1983.
Tulsa Time/Knockin' On Heaven's Door/If I Don't Be There By Morning/ Rambling On My Mind/Presence Of The Lord/Can't Find My Way Home/Smile/ Blues Power.

ERIC CLAPTON AND HIS BAND

Eric Clapton

There's one in every crowd

MARKETED BY POLYDOR LIMITED

COMPACT DISCS

Eric can be found on the following bits of 4in technology.

1. JOHN MAYALL AND THE BLUESBREAKERS FEATURING ERIC CLAPTON

2. 461 OCEAN BOULEVARD

3. JUST ONE NIGHT

4. TIME PIECES

5. MONEY AND CIGARETTES

6. CHRISTINE McVIE
Christine McVie.

7. THE PROS AND CONS OF HITCH-HIKING
Roger Waters.

45

Seasonal Greetings
from

THE ROBERT STIGWOOD ORGANISATION LTD

67 BROOK STREET

LONDON W1
Tel - 629 9121

PP Arnold, Babylon, Ginger Baker, Cliff Bennett,
Graham Bonnet, Jack Bruce, Eric Clapton, Cream,
Jackie Edwards, Blind Faith, Georgie Fame,
Chris Farlowe, Barry Maurice Gibb, Rick Grech,
Billy M. Lawrie, Fat Mattress, John Mayall,
Glass Menagerie, Eric Mercury, Zoot Money,
Paul Nicholas, Poet and One Man Band,
Alan Price, Atomic Rooster, Samantha Sang,
The Slade, Taste, Tintin, Ferris Wheel.

PROMO RECORDS

1. ERIC CLAPTON ON WHITE
RSO PRO 035, white vinyl (12″).
Released November 1977 for promotion only to various radio stations.
   Side One: Cocaine (Cale)/The Core (Levy, Clapton).
   Side Two: Lay Down Sally (Levy, Clapton)/Wonderful Tonight (Clapton).
   All tracks from 'Slowhand'.

2. ERIC CLAPTON SPECIAL 12″ AOR DISC
RSO RPO 1005 (12″).
Released November 1978.
   Side One: Promises (Feldman, Linn).

Side Two: Watch Out For Lucy (Clapton).
   Both tracks from 'Backless'.

3. ERIC CLAPTON LIMITED BACKLESS (with picture label of Eric playing guitar)
RSO RPO 1009 (12″).
Released November 1978.
   Side One: Watch Out For Lucy (Clapton)/I'll Make Love To You Anytime (Cale)/Roll It (Levy, Clapton).
   Side Two: Promises (Feldman, Linn)/If I Don't Be There By Morning (Dylan)/Tell Me That You Love Me (Clapton).

4. ERIC CLAPTON LIMITED NUMBERED EDITION OF 1000
No code (12″).
Released May 1980.
   Side One: Wonderful Tonight (Clapton).
   Side Two: Further On Up The Road (Veasy, Robey).
   Both tracks from 'Just One Night'.

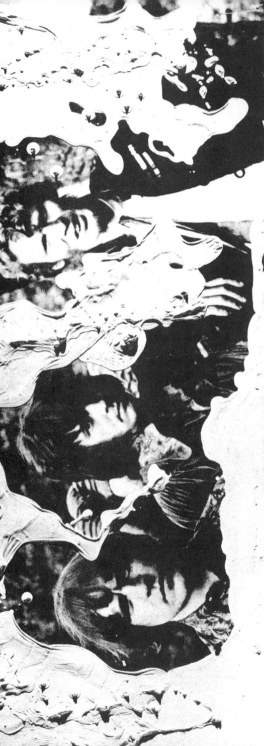

THE **CREAM'S L.P.** IS RELEASED ON DECEMBER 9TH. THE TITLE IS **'FRESH CREAM'**
THEIR SECOND SINGLE IS ALSO RELEASED ON THE SAME DAY- IT IS CALLED **'I FEEL FREE'**
THE FLIP: **'N.S.U.'** - BOTH ON

SINGLE: 591 011/THE L.P.:593 001 (MONO) & 594 001 (STEREO)

MANAGED & DISTRIBUTED BY POLYDOR RECORDS LTD. FOR THE ROBERT STIGWOOD ORGANISATION.

BOOTLEGS

THE YARDBIRDS

1. BOOM BOOM/HONEY IN HER HIPS
(Single).
BUZZ 101.

2. MORE GOLDEN EGGS
(LP).
TMOQ 61003.
Eric only appears on a longer version of 'I Wish You Would'.

CREAM

1. TOP OF THE MILK
(EP).
MTGL 332788.
Steppin' Out/Big Black Woman Blues/Lawdy Mama/Crossroads.

2. HELLO AGAIN ON TOUR
(LP).
ZAP 7865.
Steppin' Out/Sweet Wine/Lost Love/ N.S.U./Big Mama Blues/Sleepy Time Time/Crossroads.

3. ROYAL ALBERT HALL, 1968
(LP).
WRMB 366.
Cat Squirrel/Hey Lawdy Mama/ Spoonful/Crossroads/N.S.U./White Room/Sunshine Of Your Love.

4. '67 – '68
(LP).
CMB47-106.
Steppin' Out/Sweet Wine/Lost Love/ N.S.U./Big Black Woman Blues/Sleepy Time Time/Crossroads. All from Amsterdam, 1967.
White Room/Politician/Crossroads/ Sitting On Top Of The World/I'm So Glad/ Sunshine Of Your Love. All from Albert Hall, 1968.

BLIND FAITH

1. US TOUR
(LP).
TAKRL 1902.
Crossroads/Presence Of The Lord/ Means To An End/Well Alright/Can't Find My Way Home/Had To Cry Today.

DEREK AND THE DOMINOS

1. STORMY MONDAY
(LP).
TMOQ 71082.
Recorded live at Santa Monica Civic, November 20, 1970.
Derek's Boogie/Blues Power/Stormy Monday/Let It Rain.

ERIC CLAPTON

1. GEORGIA PEACH
(LP).
FLAT 8223.
Recorded live in Dallas, November 1976.

Hello Old Friend/Badge/Knocking On Heaven's Door/One Night With You/Tell The Truth/Can't Find My Way Home/ Blues Power.

2. AN ELECTRIC COLLECTION, 1974 TOUR, VOL. 1
(LP).
ZAP 7851.
Easy Now/Let It Grow/I Shot The Sheriff/Layla/Smile/Little Wing/Willie And The Hand Jive/Get Ready.

3. AN ELECTRIC COLLECTION, 1974 TOUR, VOL. 2
(LP).
ZAP 7852.
Both LPs were recorded at Long Beach Arena,July 20, 1974.
Badge/Can't Find My Way Home/ Driftin' And Driftin'/Let It Rain/Presence Of The Lord/Crossroads/Steady Rollin' Man/Little Queenie.

4. HAND JIVE
(LP).
ZAP 7884.
Recorded live in Boston, July 12, 1974, and in Providence, July10, 1974.
Willie And The Hand Jive/Get Ready/ Untitled/Layla/Little Queenie/Badge/ Layla.

5. SLOWHAND IN BOSTON
(LP).
ZAP 7880.
Recorded July 12, 1974.
Smile/Have You Ever Been Lonely?/ Have You Ever Loved A Woman?/Blues Power/Can't Find My Way Home/ Presence Of The Lord/Bright Lights Big City.

6. SMILE
(LP).
ZAP 7881.
Recorded live in Providence, July 10, 1974.
Smile/Let It Grow/Willie And The Hand Jive/Layla/Blues Power/Little Queenie.

7. 74
(LP).
Berkeley Records.
Recorded live at Madison Square Garden, July 13, 1974.
Can't Find My Way Home/Willie And The Hand Jive/Layla/Presence Of The Lord/Blues Power/Badge.

8. LIVE IN LONDON
(LP).
Caution Music.
Recorded in fact in Germany, 1974.
I Shot The Sheriff/Little Rachel/Let It Grow/Get Ready/Badge/Layla/Dream Dream Dream.

9. SNOWHEAD
(LP).
EC 1978.
Recorded live in Santa Monica, February 1978, and in Dallas, 1976.
Knocking On Heaven's Door/Lay Down Sally/Next Time You See Her/ Cocaine/Badge/Sign Language/Layla.

10. R 'N' R HEART
(LP).
Scorpio Records.
Recorded live in Genoa, Italy, May 3, 1983.
I Shot The Sheriff/Worried Life Blues/ Key To The Highway/After Midnight/The Shape You're In/Wonderful Tonight/ Cocaine/Further On Up The Road.
Limited edition of 1000.

11. THE SHAPE YOU'RE IN
(LP).
Tulsa Time/I Shot The Sheriff/ Lay Down Sally/Worried Life Blues/Let It Rain/Double Trouble/ Sweet Little Lisa/Key To The Highway/After Midnight/The Shape You're In/Wonderful Tonight/Blues Power/Ramblin' On My Mind/Have You Ever Loved A Woman?/ Cocaine/Layla/Further On Up The Road. All recorded at The Sporthalle, Cologne, April 26, 1983.
Blow Wind Blow/Motherless Children/Whiter Shade Of Pale/ Setting Me Up/Another Ticket/ Badge. All recorded Kyoto 1981.
Treble LP from Japan, limited to 500.

OTHER BOOTLEGS WHERE EC CAN BE FOUND

1. BROWN SUGAR
Rolling Stones (Single).
Hard On Records.

2. LOOSE CABOOSE
Bonzo Dog Band (LP).
TAKRL 1922.
   Eric only plays on 'Paper Round'.

3. ROCK AND ROLL CIRCUS
(LP).
Phonygraf.
   Eric only plays on 'Yer Blues', with
John Lennon, Mitch Mitchell, Keith
Richards.

4. BANGLA DESH CONCERTS
   Various LPs came out from the two
concerts afternoon and evening.

5. DELANEY AND BONNIE WITH ERIC CLAPTON AND GEORGE HARRISON
CBM 4450.
Recorded live at the Falkoner,
Copenhagen, 1969.
   Oh Lord/I Don't Know Why/Those
Who Will/Special Life/You're My
Girl/Someone/Coming Home/Tutti Frutti.

DORIS TROY'S
Album is OUT NOW on Apple Records

SAPCOR 13

SESSION WORK

From the early days to the present, Eric has contributed to many sessions both live and in the studio.

1. THE BLUES OF OTIS SPANN
Otis Spann (LP).
UK LP Decca.
Eric plays on 'Pretty Girls Everywhere', UK Single Decca F11972, and on 'Stirs Me Up'.
Recorded May 1964.
Personnel: Muddy Waters guitar, vocals. Ransome Knowling bass. Willie Smith drums. Eric Clapton guitar.

2. FROM NEW ORLEANS TO CHICAGO
Champion Jack Dupree (LP).
UK Decca LK4747.
USA London PS553.
Released April 1966.
Recorded late 1965.
Eric plays on Calcutta Blues/ Shim-Sham-Shimmy/Third Degree.
Personnel: Keef Hartley drums. Malcolm Pool bass. Tony McPhee guitar. Eric Clapton guitar.

3. ANTHOLOGY OF BRITISH BLUES, VOLUMES 1 AND 2
UK LP IMAL 03/04 and IMAL 05/06.
Released 1968.
In between The Yardbirds and John Mayall, Eric did a few tracks with Jimmy Page and various members of The Rolling Stones. The tracks with just JP are Draggin' My Tail/Choker/Miles Road/ Long Hard Road.
The other tracks are Snake Drive/ Tribute To Elmore/West Coast Idea, which also featured: Mick Jagger harmonica. Bill Wyman bass. Ian Stewart piano. Chris Winters drums.

54

4. WE'RE ONLY IN IT FOR THE MONEY
The Mothers Of Invention (LP).
UK Verve VLP 9199.
USA V65045X.
Released June 1968.
Produced by Frank Zappa.
　　Eric plays and cries out "God, it's God, I see God" on 'Nasal Retentive Calliope Music'.

5. LADY SOUL
Aretha Franklin (LP).
UK Atlantic K40016.
Released March 1968.
Produced by Jerry Wexler.
　　Eric plays on 'Good To Me As I Am To You'.

6. WONDERWALL MUSIC
George Harrison (LP).
UK Apple SAPCOR 1.
USA ST 3350.

Released November 1968.
Produced by George Harrison.
　　Eric plays on 'Ski-ing'.

7. WHITE ALBUM
The Beatles (LP).
UK Apple PMC/PCS 7067/7068.
USA SWBO 101.
Released November 1968.
　　Eric plays on 'While My Guitar Gently Weeps'.
　　Personnel: George Harrison guitar, vocals. Eric Clapton guitar solo. Paul McCartney bass. Ringo Starr drums.

8. IS THIS WHAT YOU WANT?
Jackie Lomax (LP).
UK Apple SAPCOR 6.
USA ST3354.
Released 1969.
　　Eric plays on Sour Milk Sea/The Eagle Laughs At You.
　　Personnel: Jackie Lomax vocals. George Harrison guitar. Ringo Starr drums. Eric Clapton guitar. Nicky Hopkins piano.

9. FLY
Yoko Ono (LP).
UK Apple SAPTU 101/2.
Released December 1971.
    Eric plays on 'Don't Worry Kyoko'.
    Personnel: Yoko Ono vocals. John
Lennon guitar. Klaus Voormann bass.
Eric Clapton guitar. Ringo Starr drums.

Eric plays on Do What You Want/
That's The Way God Planned It.
    Other musicians include Ringo Starr,
George Harrison, Doris Troy, Ginger
Baker.

10. ENCOURAGING WORDS
Billy Preston (LP).
UK Apple SAPCOR 14.
USA ST3359.
Released 1969.
    Eric plays on Right Now/Use What
You've Got/I Don't Want To Pretend/
Encouraging Words.

11. CONTRIBUTION
Shawn Phillips (LP).
USA A&M SP4241.
Released January 1970.
    Eric plays on 'Man Hole Covered
Wagon'.
    Personnel: Steve Winwood organ.
Mick Weaver piano. John Carr conga.
Eric Clapton guitar. Shawn Phillips guitar,
vocals.

12. FIENDS AND ANGELS
Martha Velez (LP).
UK SHK 8395.
USA Sire SES 97008.
Released 1969.
    Eric plays on 'I'm Gonna Leave You'.
    Personnel: Jack Bruce bass. Mitch
Mitchell drums. Jim Capaldi drums. Eric
Clapton guitar. Duster Bennet guitar. Paul
Kossoff guitar.

13. THAT'S THE WAY GOD
PLANNED IT
Billy Preston (LP).
UK Apple SAPCOR 9.
Released 1969.

14. LEON RUSSELL
Leon Russell (LP).
UK A&M AMLS 982.
USA SRL 52007.
Released May 1970.
    Eric plays on I Put A Spell On You/
Shoot Out On The Plantation/Delta Lady/
Prince Of Peace/Hurtsome Body/Roll
Away The Stone.
    Personnel: Leon Russell piano, guitar,
vocals. Chris Stainton keyboard. Jim
Price sax. Carl Radle bass. Jim Gordon
drums. George Harrison guitar. Ringo
Starr drums. Bill Wyman bass. Charlie
Watts drums.
    Also various other superstar names of
the time such as Joe Cocker, Stevie
Winwood, Delaney and Bonnie Bramlett.

15. LEON RUSSELL AND THE SHELTER PEOPLE
Leon Russell (LP).
UK A&M AMLS 65003.
USA SRL 52008.
Released June 1971.
    Eric plays on Alcatraz/Beware Of Darkness.
    Personnel: Leon Russell piano, guitar, vocals. Chris Stainton keyboard. Jim Price trumpet. Carl Radle bass. Jim Gordon drums.

16. DORIS TROY
Doris Troy (LP).
UK Apple SAPCOR 13.
USA ST3371.
Released September 1970.
    Eric plays on Ain't That Cute/Give Me Back My Dynamite/You Tore Me Up Inside/I've Got To Be Strong/So Far/You Give Me Joy Joy/Don't Call Me No More/Jacob's Ladder.

    Personnel: Doris Troy vocals. Ringo Starr drums. Klaus Voorman bass. Billy Preston organ, vocals. George Harrison guitar. Eric Clapton guitar.
    On 'You Tore Me Up Inside' Alan White plays drums.
    On 'You Give Me Joy Joy' Eric Clapton plays rhythm guitar, Steve Stills plays the first guitar solo and Peter Frampton plays the second.

17. THE WORST OF
Ashton Gardner and Dyke (LP).
UK EMI E-ST563.
Released 1971.
    Eric plays on 'I'm Your Spiritual Breadman'.
    Personnel: George Harrison electric swivel guitar. Eric Clapton lead guitar. Tony Ashton keyboards, vocals. Kim Gardner bass. Roy Dyke drums.

18. STEPHEN STILLS
Stephen Stills (LP).
UK Atlantic 2401004.
USA Atlantic SD 7202.
Released November 1970.
    Eric plays on 'Go Back Home'.
    Personnel: Stephen Stills guitar, keyboard, vocals. Eric Clapton 2nd lead guitar. Calvin Samuels bass. Dallas Taylor drums.

19. 2
Stephen Stills (LP).
UK Atlantic 2401013.
USA Atlantic SD 7206.
Released July 1971.
    Eric plays on 'Fishes And Scorpions'.
    Personnel: Stephen Stills guitar, vocals. Eric Clapton lead guitar. Calvin Samuels bass. Dallas Taylor drums.

20. PLAY THE BLUES
Buddy Guy and Junior Wells (LP).
UK Atlantic K40240.

USA Atco SD 33-364.
Released 1972.

Eric plays on A Man Of Many Words/My Baby She Left Me (She Left Me A Mule To Ride)/Come On In This House – Have Mercy Baby/T-Bone Shuffle/A Poor Man's Plea/Messin' With The Kid/I Don't Know/Bad Bad Whiskey.

Personnel: Junior Wells vocals, harmonica. Buddy Guy vocals, lead and rhythm guitar. Eric Clapton rhythm and bottleneck guitar. A.C. Reed tenor sax. Mike Utley piano, organ. Leroy Stewart bass. Roosevelt Shaw drums.

On 'A Man Of Many Words' Carl Radle and Jim Gordon replace Leroy Stewart and Roosevelt Shaw on bass and drums respectively.

On A Man Of Many Words/T-Bone Shuffle/Messin' With The Kid, Dr John replaces Mike Utley on piano.

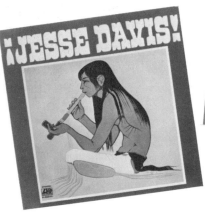

SESSION WORK

21. JESSE DAVIS
Jesse Davis (LP).
UK Atlantic 2400106.
USA Atco SD 35-346.
Released 1971.

Eric plays on Reno Street Incident/Tulsa County/Washita Love Child/Every Night Is Saturday Night/You Bella Donna You/Rock And Roll Gypsies/Golden Sun Goddess/Crazy Love.

Personnel: Joel Scott Hill guitar. Eric Clapton guitar. Larry Knechtel, Larry Pierce, Leon Russell, Ben Sidran, John Simon keyboards. Billy Rich, Steve Thompson bass. Chuck Blackwell, Steve Mitchell, Bruce Rowland, Alan White drums. Patt Daley, Sandy Konikoff, Jackie Lomax, Pete Waddington, Johnnie Ware, Alan Yoshida percussion. James Gordon, Jerry Jumonville, Darrell Leonard, Frank Mayes horns. Nikki Barclay, Merry Clayton, Vanetta Fields, Bobby Jones,

Gloria Jones, Clydie King, Gram Parsons, Maxine Willard vocal accompanists.

22. LABIO-DENTAL FRICATIVE (Stanshall)/PAPER ROUND (Stanshall)
Vivian Stanshall (Single).
UK Liberty LBF 15309.
Released 1970.

Great guitar playing on these two tracks which are now sadly deleted. However, a remixed version of the A-side can be found on 'History Of The Bonzos', United Artists UAD60071/2, which was released in 1974.

23. SUN MOON AND HERBS
Dr John (LP).
UK Atlantic 2400161.
US ATCO SD 33-362.
Released November 1971.
Atlantic K40250. Reissue 1972.

Eric plays on Black John The Conqueror/Where Ya At Mule?/Craney Crow/Pots On Fiyo (File Gumbo) – Who I Got To Fall On (If The Pot Get Heavy)?/ Zu Zu Mamou/Familiar Reality – Reprise.

Personnel: Dr John vocals, piano, organ, guitar, vibes, percussion. Eric Clapton slide guitar. Tommy Feronne rhythm guitar. Vic Brox pocket trumpet, organ. Ray Draper tuba, percussion, backing vocals. Fred Staehle trap drums. Mick Jagger, Shirley Goodman, Tammi Lynn, P.P. Arnold, Joni Jonz backing vocals.

24. THE LONDON SESSIONS
Howlin' Wolf (LP).
UK Rolling Stones COC 49101.
USA Chess CH 60008.
Released 1971.

Eric plays on Rockin' Daddy/I Ain't Superstitious/Sittin' On Top Of The World/Worried About My Baby/What A

Woman/Poor Boy/Built For Comfort/
Who's Been Talking?/The Red Rooster/
Do The Do/Highway 49/Wang – Dang –
Doodle.

Personnel: Howlin' Wolf vocals,
harmonica, acoustic guitar. Eric Clapton
lead guitar. Stevie Winwood piano, organ.
Bill Wyman bass. Charlie Watts drums.
Hubert Sumlin rhythm guitar. Jeffrey M.
Carp harmonica. Ian Stewart piano.

Additional personnel: Ringo Starr
drums on 'I Ain't Superstitious'. Klaus
Voorman bass on 'I Ain't Superstitious'.
John Simon piano on 'Who's Been
Talking?'. Phil Upchurch bass on 'Rockin'
Daddy'. Lafayette Leake piano on 'Sittin'
On Top Of The World', 'Worried About My
Baby' and 'The Red Rooster'. Joe Miller,
Jordan Sandke, Dennis Lansing horns
on 'I Ain't Superstitious' and 'Built For
Comfort'.

25. LONDON REVISITED
Muddy Waters and Howlin' Wolf (LP).
Chess 60028. US release only.
Released 1974.

Eric plays on the Howlin' Wolf side
which is basically outtakes from 'The
London Sessions'.

Tracks are Goin' Down Slow/The
Killing Floor/I Want To Have A Word With
You.

Personnel: same as 'The London
Sessions'.

26. BOBBY KEYS
Bobby Keys (LP).
Warner Bros K46141.
Released 1972.

Eric plays on Steal From A King/
Bootleg/Command Performance/Crispy
Duck.

Personnel: Bobby Keys sax. Jim Price
trumpet. Jim Gordon drums. Dave Mason
guitar. Eric Clapton guitar. George
Harrison guitar. Klaus Voormann bass.

27. BOBBY WHITLOCK
Bobby Whitlock (LP).
UK CBS S65109.
USA Dunhill DSX 50121.
Released 1972.

Eric plays on Where There's A Will
There's A Way/A Day Without Jesus/
Back In My Life Again/The Scenery Has
Slowly Changed.

Personnel includes: Bobby Whitlock
keyboards, guitar, vocals. George
Harrison guitar. Eric Clapton guitar. Klaus
Voormann bass. Jim Gordon drums. Carl
Radle bass. Jim Keltner drums.

28. RAW VELVET
Bobby Whitlock (LP).
UK CBS 65301.
USA Dunhill DSX 50131.
Released 1972.

Eric plays on Hello L.A. Bye Bye Birmingham/The Dreams Of A Hobo.

Personnel: Bobby Whitlock rhythm guitar, vocals. Carl Radle bass. Jim Gordon drums. Eric Clapton lead and slide guitar. Delaney Bramlett background vocals.

'Dreams Of A Hobo' was, in fact, on the US LP 'Bobby Whitlock' but left off the British release.

29. ALL THINGS MUST PASS (Triple Set)

George Harrison (LP).
UK Apple STCH 639.
USA STCH 639.
Released November 1970.

Eric plays on I'd Have You Anytime/My Sweet Lord/Wah Wah/Isn't It A Pity? (Version One)/What Is Life?/If Not For You/Behind That Locked Door/Let It Down/Run Of The Mill/Beware Of Darkness/Apple Scruffs/Ballad Of Sir Frankie Crisp/Awaiting On You All/All Things Must Pass/I Dig Love/Art Of Dying/Isn't It A Pity? (Version Two)/Hear Me Lord.

Personnel: George Harrison guitar, vocals. Dave Mason guitar. Eric Clapton guitar. Ringo Starr, Alan White, Jim Gordon drums. Klaus Voormann, Carl Radle bass. Gary Wright, Bobby Whitlock, Billy Preston, Gary Brooker keyboard. Pete Drake pedal steel guitar. Bobby Keys tenor sax and Jim Price trumpet. Badfinger rhythm guitar and percussion. John Barham orchestral arrangements.

The third LP in this box set comprises various jams recorded during the making of this LP as follows:

'Out Of The Blue'.

Personnel: Jim Gordon, Carl Radle, Bobby Whitlock, Eric Clapton, Gary Wright, George Harrison, Jim Price, Bobby Keys, Al Aronowitz.

'Plug Me In' and 'Thanks For The Pepperoni'.

Personnel: Jim Gordon, Carl Radle, Bobby Whitlock, Eric Clapton, Dave Mason, George Harrison.

'I Remember Jeep'.

Personnel: Ginger Baker, Klaus Voormann, Billy Preston, Eric Clapton, George Harrison.

The withdrawn Derek and The Dominos single 'Tell The Truth' B/W 'Roll It Over' was recorded during the above sessions.

30. THE CONCERT FOR BANGLA DESH

George Harrison (LP).
UK Apple STCX 3385.
USA STCX 3385.
Released January 1972.
Recorded live at Madison Square Garden, New York, August 1, 1971.

Eric plays on Wah Wah/My Sweet Lord/Awaiting On You All/That's The Way God Planned It/It Don't Come Easy/Beware Of Darkness/While My Guitar Gently Weeps/Jumpin' Jack Flash/Young Blood/Something/Bangla Desh.

Personnel: George Harrison guitar, vocals. Eric Clapton guitar. Billy Preston keyboard, vocals. Leon Russell piano, vocals. Ringo Starr drums. Jesse Ed Davis guitar. Klaus Voormann bass. Jim Keltner drums. Carl Radle bass. Badfinger acoustic guitars, backing vocals.

Also Don Preston guitar on Jumpin' Jack Flash/Young Blood.

31. BACK TO THE ROOTS

John Mayall (LP).

UK Polydor 2657 005.
USA Polydor 25.3002.
Released June 1971.
　　Eric plays on Prisons On The Road/
Accidental Suicide/Home Again/Looking
At Tomorrow/Force Of Nature/Goodbye
December.

32. ANTHOLOGY
Duane Allman (LP).
UK Capricorn 2659035.
USA 2CP 0108.
Released 1972.
Recorded around the time of the 'Layla'
sessions, at Criteria Studios, Miami,
October 1970.
　　Eric plays on 'Mean Old World'.
　　Personnel: Eric Clapton guitar. Duane
Allman guitar.
　　Original copies included a free
booklet which contained a photo of
above session.

33. ROCKIN' 50'S ROCK 'N' ROLL
The Crickets (LP).
UK CBS 64301.
Released February 1971.
　　Eric plays on Rockin' 50's Rock And
Roll/That'll Be The Day.
　　Personnel: Sonny Curtis vocals. Eric
Clapton guitar, vocals. Delaney Bramlett
guitar, vocals. Jerry Allison vocals. Carl
Radle bass. Jim Gordon drums. Bonnie
Bramlett vocals.
　　Eric had wanted to do an album of
Buddy Holly classics, but this is as far as
the project went.

34. DON'T YOU BELIEVE IT (Kelly)
Jonathan Kelly (Single).
UK Parlophone R5851.
Released 1970.
　　Jonathan Kelly in Zigzag 31: "Eric
Clapton played slide on 'Don't You
Believe it'. Colin (Peterson) used to work
for Stigwood and I guess he met the

Cream guys when he was in the office,
and he asked him if he'd come and play
on a twelve bar, and he just turned up,
which blew my mind. He listened to the
backing tracks and bang, just played it."
　　Eric is not featured on B-side.

35. BANGLA DESH (Harrison)/DEEP BLUE
George Harrison (Single).
Apple R5912.
Released July 1971.
　　A-side personnel: George Harrison
guitar, vocals. Ringo Starr drums. Eric
Clapton guitar. Bobby Keys sax. Billy
Preston organ. Leon Russell piano.
　　B-side personnel: George Harrison
guitar, vocals. Eric Clapton guitar. Ringo
Starr drums.

36. TEASIN'
King Curtis (Single).
USA Atco 2091 012.
Released 1970.
　　One of Eric's favourite sessions.
　　Personnel: King Curtis sax. Eric
Clapton lead guitar. Delaney Bramlett
acoustic and rhythm guitars. Jim Gordon
drums. Carl Radle bass.
　　Can also be found on LP 'Get Ready',
Atco 33338.

37. BURGLAR
Freddie King (LP).
UK RSO 2394 140.
USA SO 4803.
Released 1975.
　　Eric plays on 'Sugar Sweet'.
　　Personnel: Freddie King vocals, guitar.
Eric Clapton guitar. George Terry guitar.
Dick Sims organ. Carl Radle bass. Jamie
Oldaker drums.

38. 1934-1976
Freddie King (LP).

SESSION WORK

UK RSO 2394 192.
USA RS-1-3025.
Released 1976.
 Eric plays on Sugar Sweet/TV Mama/
Gambling Woman Blues/Further Up The
Road.
 Personnel as on 'Burglar' plus Sergio
Pastora percussion on 'Further On Up
The Road'.

39. HOLLYWOOD BE THY NAME
Dr John (LP).
UK United Artists UAG 29902.
USA UALA 552-G.
Released December 1975.
 Eric plays congas on 'Reggae Doctor'.

40. RICK DANKO
Rick Danko (LP).
UK Arista SIART 1037.
USA AB4141.
Released 1978.
 Eric plays on 'New Mexico'.
 Personnel: Rick Danko bass, vocals.
Rob Frabont tambourine. Garth Hudson
accordion. Eric Clapton guitar solo.

41. THE LAST WALTZ
The Band (LP).
UK Warner Bros K66076.
USA 3WS 3146.
Released April 1978.
 Eric plays on Further On Up The
Road/I Shall Be Released. Recorded live
at The Band's last ever concert with a
cast of thousands including Van
Morrison, Ringo Starr, Joni Mitchell, Bob
Dylan, Neil Diamond, Neil Young, Dr
John.
 Eric also played on 'All Our Pastimes'
which is not included on the LP, as well
as appearing alongside Ronnie Wood,
Neil Young, Carl Radle, Steve Stills,
Robbie Robertson, Ringo Starr for a long
blues jam at the end of the concert.

42. DARK HORSE
George Harrison (LP).
UK Apple PAS 10008.
Released December 1974.
 Eric supposedly plays on 'Bye Bye
Love' and is credited as such, but denies
this in an interview in Rolling Stone,
November 20, 1975 issue.

43. LASSO FROM EL PASO
Kinky Friedman (LP).
USA Epic 34304.
Released 1976.
 Eric plays on Kinky/Ol' Ben Lucas.
 Personnel: Kinky Friedman vocals,
guitar. Eric Clapton dobro. Rick Danko
bass. Levon Helm drums. Dr John toy
piano on 'Ol' Ben Lucas'. Al Garth fiddle
on 'Ol' Ben Lucas'. Ron Wood guitar on
'Kinky'.

44. DESIRE
Bob Dylan (LP).
UK CBS 86003.
Released December 1975.
 Eric plays on 'Romance in Durango'.
 Eric had in fact contributed to the
whole LP alongside various members of
Kokomo, but Bob Dylan decided he was
unhappy with the sound and re-recorded
the whole LP, except for the above
mentioned track.

45. TOMMY (Soundtrack)
UK Polydor 2335093.
USA PD 29502.
Released 1975.
 Eric plays on Eyesight To The Blind/
Sally Simpson.
 Personnel on 'Eyesight To The Blind':
Kenny Jones drums. John Entwistle bass.
Eric Clapton vocals, guitar.
 Personnel on 'Sally Simpson': Phil
Chen bass. Nicky Hopkins piano. Eric
Clapton guitar. Graham Deakin drums.
Pete Townshend, Roger Daltrey vocals.

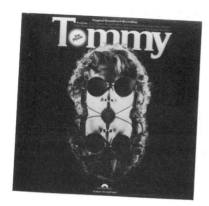

46. ROTOGRAVURE
Ringo Starr (LP).
UK Polydor 2302040.
USA Atlantic SD 18193.
Released October 1976.
Eric plays on 'This Be Called A Song' which he also wrote.
Personnel: Eric Clapton guitar. Lon Van Eaton guitar. Klaus Voormann bass. Ringo Starr drums. Jim Keltner drums. Jane Getz piano. Melissa Manchester, Vini Poncia, Joe Bean backing vocals. Robert Greenidge steel drums.

47. FIRST ALBUM
Arthur Louis (LP).
Polydor MP 2547. Japanese release only.
Released 1976.
Eric plays on The Dealer/Come On And Love Me/Train 444/Go And Make It Happen/Plum/Knocking On Heaven's Door/Still It Feels Good.
Personnel: Arthur Louis guitar, vocals. Robert Bailey keyboards, synthesizer.

Richard Bailey drums. Winstone Deleando guitar. Peter Dafrey bass. Ernestine Pierce vocals. Eric Clapton lead guitar. Gene Chandler vocals on 'The Dealer'.
Various singles were released in the UK:
(i) KNOCKING ON HEAVEN'S DOOR/ PLUM
Plum PIP 0001.
(ii) KNOCKING ON HEAVEN'S DOOR/ THE DEALER
Island WIP 6448.
(iii) STILL IT FEELS GOOD/COME ON AND LOVE ME
Mainstreet MS 104.

48. GEORGE HARRISON
George Harrison (LP).
UK Dark Horse K56562.
USA Capitol SN 16055.
Released 1979.
Eric plays on 'Love Comes To Everyone'.
Personnel: George Harrison guitars, vocals. Andy Newmark bass. Willie Weeks bass. Neil Larsen keyboards, mini Moog. Steve Winwood various Moogs, backing vocals.

49. MAKIN' IT ON THE STREET
Corky Laing (LP).
USA Elektra 7E 1097.
Released 1977.
Eric plays on 'On My Way (By The River)'.
Personnel: Corky Laing vocals, drums. Neil Larsen keyboards. George Terry guitar. Eric Clapton guitar. Calvin Arline bass.

50.STINGRAY
Joe Cocker (LP).
UK A&M AMLH 64574.
USA SP 4574.
Released June 1976.
Eric plays on 'Worrier'.

Personnel: Joe Cocker vocals. Eric Clapton guitar. Bonnie Bramlett backing vocals. Cornell Dupree guitar. Steve Gadd drums. Richard Tee keyboards. Gordon Edwards bass. Eric Gale guitar.

51. MUSIC FROM FREE CREEK
UK Charisma CAD5101-2.
Released 1973.
Eric plays on Road Song/Getting Back To Molly/No One Knows.

Personnel on 'Road Song': Doctor John guitar. Eric Clapton guitar. Moogy Klingman organ. Richard Crooks drums. Stu Woods bass. Delaney Bramlett rhythm guitar. Tommy Cosgrove vocals.

Personnel on 'Getting Back To Molly': as above plus Earle Doud vocals and Maretha Stewart, Hilda Harris, Valerie Simpson background vocals.

Personnel on 'No One Knows': as above plus Eric Mercury vocals, brass section.

These songs result from a massive jam session at the record plant in New York which was probably recorded in 1971.

52. THE PARTY ALBUM
Alexis Korner (LP).
Intercord 170000, Germany only.
Released 1980.
Recorded at the Gatsby Rooms, Pinewood Studios, April 28, 1978, to celebrate Alexis' 50th birthday.
Eric plays on Hey Pretty Mama/ Hi-Heel Sneakers/Stormy Monday Blues.

Personnel: Alexis Korner, Eric Clapton, Mel Collins, Chris Farlowe, Neil Ford, Dick Heckstall-Smith, Colin Hodgkinson, Paul Jones, Zoot Money, Dick Morrissey, Duffy Power, Stu Spear, John Surman, Art Themen, Mike Zwerin.

53. ONE OF THE BOYS
Roger Daltrey (LP).
UK Polydor 2442146.

USA MCA 2271.
Released May 1977.
Although Eric is credited, the story goes that Roger Daltrey brought in a large barrel of beer as a present for the various musicians who proceeded to consume said beverage before the session, and as a result all got too drunk to play and Eric was unable to return at a later date due to other commitments.

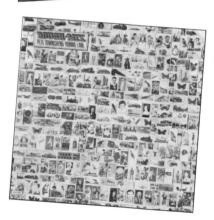

54. ROUGH MIX
Ronnie Lane, Pete Townshend (LP).
UK Polydor 2442147.
Released September 1977.
Eric plays on 'Rough Mix'.
Personnel: Pete Townshend guitar. Ronnie Lane bass. Rabbit organ. Henry Spinetti drums. Eric Clapton lead guitar.

Personnel on 'Annie': Graham Lyle 12 string acoustic guitar. Benny Gallagher accordion. Charlie Hart violin. Dave Marquee string bass. Eric Clapton 6 string acoustic. Pete Townshend and Ronnie Lane vocals.

Personnel on 'April Fool': Pete Townshend guitar. Ronnie Lane vocals. Eric Clapton dobro. Dave Marquee double basses.

Personnel on 'Till The Rivers Run Dry': Henry Spinetti drums. Box Burrell bass. Pete Townshend guitar. Ronnie Lane vocals. Eric Clapton dobro. John Entwistle, Billy Nicholls vocals.

Go To College.

Personnel: Chris Stainton keyboards. Stephen Bishop acoustic guitar. Clive Anstree cello on 'Little Moon'. Eric Clapton guitar. Phil Collins drums. John Giblun bass. Gary Brooker keyboards.

55. NIGHT EYES
Danny Douma (LP).
USA Warner Bros BSK 3326.
Released 1979.
Eric plays on 'Hate You'.
Personnel: Mick Fleetwood drums. John McVie bass. Christine McVie keyboards. Danny Douma vocals, guitar. Eric Clapton lead guitar.

56. CARELESS
Stephen Bishop (LP).
UK ABC ABCL 5201.
USA ABC 9022-954.
Released 1976.
Eric plays on 'Sinking In An Ocean Of Tears'.
Personnel: Stephen Bishop acoustic guitars, vocals. Eric Clapton electric slide guitar. Jay Graydon electric guitar. Mac Cridlin bass. Barlow Jarvis piano. Larry Brown drums. Ray Rizzi sax. Alan Lindgren synthesizers.
Personnel on 'Save It For A Rainy Day': Stephen Bishop acoustic guitars. Jeffrey Staton guitar. Eric Clapton guitar solo. Barlow Jarvis piano. Jeffrey Staton bass. Russ Kunkel drums. Chaka Khan backing vocals.

57. RED CAB TO MANHATTAN
Stephen Bishop (LP).
UK Warner Bros K56853.
USA BSK 3473.
Released 1980.
Eric plays on Little Moon/Sex Kittens

58. GLORIOUS FOOL
John Martyn (LP).
UK WEA K99178.
Released October 1981.
Eric plays on 'Couldn't Love You More'.
Personnel: John Martyn vocals, guitar. Eric Clapton guitar. Phil Collins drums. Alan Thomson bass. Max Middleton keyboards. Danny Cummings percussion.

59. LOST IN AUSTIN
Marc Benno (LP).
UK A&M AMLH 64767.
USA A&M SP-4767.
Released 1979.
Eric plays on Hotfoot Blues/Chasin' Rainbows/Me And A Friend Of Mine/New Romance/Last Train/Lost In Austin/Splish Splash/Monterey Pen/The Drifter/Hey There Senorita.
Personnel: Marc Benno guitar, piano, vocals. Albert Lee guitar. Eric Clapton guitars. Jim Keltner drums. Dick Sims keyboards. Carl Radle bass. Dickie Morrissey sax.

60. FACE VALUE
Phil Collins (LP).
UK Virgin V2185.
Released February 1981.
Eric plays on 'If Leaving Me Is Easy'.
Personnel: Phil Collins drums, keyboards, vocals. Eric Clapton guitar. Daryl Stuermer guitar. Alphonso Johnson bass. Don Myrick sax. Rahmlee Michael Davis, Michael Harris flugelhorns.

SESSION WORK

61. WHITE MANSIONS
White Mansions (LP).
UK A&M AMLX 64691.
USA SP-6004.
Released 1978.
Eric plays on White Trash/Kentucky Racehorse.
Personnel: Henry Spinetti drums. Dave Markee bass. Steve Cash harmonica. John Dillon acoustic guitar, piano, fiddle, dulcimer. Bernie Leadon backing vocals. Waylon Jennings acoustic guitar, backing vocals. Eric Clapton electric slide, dobro.

62. THE MUSIC
Secret Policeman's Other Ball (LP).
UK Springtime HAHA 6004.
Released 1982.
Recorded at Amnesty International's Charity Concert, September 1981.
Eric plays on 'Cause We Ended As Lovers/Farther On Up The Road/Crossroads.
Personnel: Eric Clapton guitar, vocals. Jeff Beck guitar. Simon Phillips drums. Neil Murray bass. John Etheridge guitar.
Personnel on 'I Shall Be Released': Sting lead vocals, guitar. Jeff Beck, Eric Clapton, John Etheridge, Neil Innes, Ray Russell guitars. John Altman, Chas Jankel keyboards. Mo Foster, Neil Murray bass. Simon Phillips drums. Mel Collins, Paul Cosh, Jeff Daly, Martin Drover, Digby Fairweather, Malcolm Griffiths, Mike Henry, Mark Isham horns. Sharon Campbell, Donovan, Sheena Easton, Phil Collins, Chris Cross, Bob Geldof, Micky Moody, Tom Robinson, Linda Taylor, Midge Ure backing vocals.

63. SEE ME
Ronnie Lane (LP).
UK RCA GEM LP 107.
Released 1980.
Eric plays on When Lad Has Got Money/Barcelona/Way Up Yonder.
Personnel: Ronnie Lane vocals. Eric Clapton guitars. Brian Belsham bass. Bruce Rowland drums. Alun Davis guitar. Bill Livsey piano. Ian Stewart piano. Charlie Hart strings. Steve Simpson strings. Carol Grimes backing vocals. Henry McCullough piano.

64. LEAD ME TO THE WATER
Gary Brooker (LP).
UK Mercury 6359098.
Released 1981.
Eric plays on 'Home Lovin''.
Singles released by Gary Brooker on which Eric can be found:
(i) HOME LOVIN'/CHASING THE CHOP
Mercury MEP70.
Released 1981.
(ii) LEAVE THE CANDLE/CHASING THE CHOP (Different version)

Chrysalis CHS 2396.
Released 1980.

65. CHRISTINE McVIE
Christine McVie (LP).
UK Warner Bros 925059-1.
USA 25059.1.
Released January 1984.
Eric plays on 'The Challenge'.
Personnel: Christine McVie keyboards, percussion, vocals. Todd Sharp guitar, vocals. George Hawkins bass, vocals. Steve Ferrone drums. Eric Clapton lead guitar. Ray Cooper percussion. Lindsey Buckingham guitar.

66. OLD WAVE
Ringo Starr (LP).
Bellaphon 260 16 029, German release.
Released 1983.
Eric plays on 'Everybody's In A Hurry But Me'.
Personnel: Ringo Starr vocals, drums. Eric Clapton guitar. Joe Walsh guitar. John Entwistle bass. Chris Stainton keyboard. Russell Kunkel drums. Waddy Wachtel guitar. Ray Cooper percussion.

67. THE PROS AND CONS OF HITCH-HIKING
Roger Waters (LP).
UK Harvest SHVL 2401051.
Released May 8, 1984.
Produced by Roger Waters and Michael Kamen.
Recorded at Abbey Road Studios, London.
All compositions by Roger Waters.
Side One: 1. Apparently They Were Travelling Abroad/2. Running Shoes/3. Arabs With Knives And West German Skies/4. For The First Time Today (Part 1)/5. Sexual Revolution/6. The Remains Of Love.
Side Two: 7. Go Fishing/8. For The First Time Today (Part 2)/9. Dunromin, Duncarin, Dunlivin/10. The Pros And Cons Of Hitch-hiking/11. Every Stranger's Eyes/12. The Moment Of Clarity.
Eric plays on all tracks.
Two singles were released from the album:
(i) THE PROS AND CONS OF HITCH-HIKING (Waters)/APPARENTLY THEY WERE TRAVELLING ABROAD (Waters)
Harvest HAR 5228 (7").
Released April 9, 1984.
(ii) THE PROS AND CONS OF HITCH-HIKING (Waters)/APPARENTLY THEY WERE TRAVELLING ABROAD (Waters)/RUNNING SHOES (Waters)
Harvest 12 HAR 5228 (12").
Released April 9, 1984.

68. COREY HART
Corey Hart (LP).

SESSION WORK

Released June 1984.
    Eric appears on 'Jenny Fey' (dobro, guitar).
EMI ST 17117, US only.

KNOWN STUDIO SESSIONS NOT RELEASED

1. 1969 recorded with George Harrison, Rick Grech, Denny Laine, Trevor Burton at Olympic Studios, London.

2. 1970 recorded with Jimi Hendrix, Steve Stills, Calvin Samuels, Conrad Isadore at Island Studios, London.

3. 1971 recorded A-side's worth of material as Derek and The Dominos.

4. 1972 recorded with Stevie Wonder at Air Studios, London.

5. 1976 recorded with Van Morrison and various Crusaders in Los Angeles.

6. 1979 recorded with Steve Cropper in Los Angeles.

7. 1976 recorded with Ginger Baker at Island Studios, Hammersmith.

8. There were also a lot of concerts that were recorded along the 1975 USA tour, and a concert with Muddy Waters at Dingwalls, London, 1978.

RUMOURS

Eric is strongly rumoured to be on the following LP's and although he attended the majority of the sessions there is no confirmation of the fact so his contribution may well have been left out.

1. BEGGARS' BANQUET
Rolling Stones.

2. ABBEY ROAD
The Beatles.

3. I'VE GOT MY OWN ALBUM TO DO
Ron Wood.

4. HAILE I HYMN
Injaman Levi.

5. ALONE TOGETHER
Dave Mason.

6. CLASS REUNION
Delaney Bramlett.

7. LUMPY GRAVY
Frank Zappa.

8. DIXIE FRIED
James Luther Dickinson.

9. HANDS OF JACK THE RIPPER
Lord Sutch.

10. COKEY COKEY/AWAY IN A MANGER
Colonel Doug Bogie (Single).

The Greatest Concert Of The Decade
NOW YOU CAN SEE IT AND HEAR IT... AS IF YOU WERE THERE!

THE CONCERT FOR BANGLADESH

apple presents

THE CONCERT FOR BANGLADESH U

ERIC CLAPTON · BOB DYLAN · GEORGE HARRISON · BILLY PRESTON
LEON RUSSELL · RAVI SHANKAR · RINGO STARR · KLAUS VOORMANN
BADFINGER · PETE HAM · TOM EVANS · JOEY MOLLAND
MIKE GIBBONS · ALLAN BEUTLER · JESSE ED DAVIS · CHUCK FINDLEY
MARLIN GRÉENE · JEANIE GREENE · JO GREEN · DOLORES HALL
JIM HORN · KAMALA CHAKRAVARTY · JACKIE KELSO · JIM KELTNER
USTED ALIAKBAR KHAN · CLAUDIA LENNEAR · LOU McCREARY
OLLIE MITCHELL · DON NIX · DON PRESTON · CARL RADLE · ALLA RAKAH

Directed by Saul Swimmer · Produced by George Harrison and Allen Klein

Music Recording Produced by George Harrison and Phil Spector · Technicolor"

apple / 20th century-fox release   Original Sound Track Available On Apple Records

VIDEO/FILM/ TV APPEARANCES

1. CREAM'S FAREWELL CONCERT AT THE ALBERT HALL
November 26, 1978.

2. BLIND FAITH IN HYDE PARK
June 7, 1969.
Only one song from this concert has so far been seen on television. This was on The Bee Gees special 'Cucumber Castle' along with a very small portion of 'Do What You Like' on a Dutch Stevie Winwood TV special.

3. ROLLING STONES ROCK 'N' ROLL CIRCUS
December 12, 1968.
Eric performs alongside John Lennon, Keith Richards, Mitch Mitchell on 'Yer Blues' and an instrumental.

4. SUPERSHOW
Massive jam session filmed at a film studio in Staines in 1969 with Eric playing alongside Buddy Guy, Duster Bennett, Roland Kirk, Jon Hiseman to name but a few.

5. INTERVIEW AND CONCERT FOOTAGE FROM U.S.A. 75 TOUR
For Tony Palmer's 'All You Need Is Love' series.

6. ALEXIS KORNER'S 50TH BIRTHDAY PARTY
Recorded at Pinewood Film Studios, April 1978.

7. BANGLA DESH
George Harrison's charity concert for the people of Bangla Desh recorded at Madison Square Garden, August 1971.

8. LAST WALTZ
Recorded at The Band's farewell concert in San Francisco at the Winterland, November 1976.

9. CHAS AND DAVE XMAS '82 TV SPECIAL
Eric performs 'Goodnight Irene' and 'Slow Down Linda'.

10. ERIC CLAPTON'S ROLLING HOTEL
Film of Eric's 1978 European tour featuring amongst other gems various jams between the EC Band and George Harrison, Elton John, Muddy Waters.

11. BBC BREAKFAST TV
Mike Smith interview after the Music Awards, June 24, 1983.

12. OLD GREY WHISTLE TEST
Live concert recorded at the BBC's Shepherds Bush studio, April 26, 1977.

13. SECRET POLICEMAN'S OTHER BALL
Eric performs alongside Jeff Beck at Drury Lane, September 1981.

14. TV AM
Interview featuring Eric, September 17, 1983.
Ronnie Lane and Bill Wyman talking about the forthcoming ARMS shows at the Albert Hall.

15. JIMI HENDRIX
Eric is interviewed on several occasions in this film about his friend.

JOHN & TONY SMITH PRESENT

In association with

THE ROBERT STIGWOOD ORGANISATION

DELANEY & BONNIE

AND **FRIENDS**

with **GUEST STAR**

ERIC CLAPTON

SUE & SUNNY

plus **P. P. ARNOLD**

& ASHTON, GARDENER & DYKE

Mon.,	1st Dec.	ROYAL ALBERT HALL	at 7.30
Tues.,	2nd Dec.	COLSTON HALL, BRISTOL	at 6.15 & 8.45
Wed.,	3rd Dec.	TOWN HALL, BIRMINGHAM	at 6.15 & 8.45
Thurs.,	4th Dec.	CITY HALL, SHEFFIELD	at 6.20 & 8.50
Fri.,	5th Dec.	CITY HALL, NEWCASTLE	at 6.15 & 8.45
Sat.,	6th Dec.	EMPIRE THEATRE, LIVERPOOL	at 6.45 & 9.00
Sun.,	7th Dec.	FAIRFIELD HALL, CROYDON	at 6.15 & 8.35

THE LIVE TAPES

CREAM

1. SATURDAY CLUB
January 19, 1967.

2. SATURDAY CLUB
February 16, 1967.

3. SATURDAY CLUB
July 6, 1967.

4. TOP GEAR
November 2, 1967.

5. TOP GEAR
November 15, 1967.

6. TOP GEAR
December 1967.

7. TOP GEAR
February 29, 1968.

8. STOCKHOLM
April 5, 1967.

9. PSYCHEDELIC SUPERMARKET, BOSTON
September 1967.

10. BACK BAY THEATER, BOSTON
April 5, 1968.

11. BRANDEIS UNIVERSITY, WALTHAM, MASS.
April 1968.

12. SAN JOSE CIVIC CENTRE, SAN JOSE
May 25, 1968.

13. OAKDALE THEATRE, WALLINGFORD, CT.
June 15, 1968.

14. ALBUQUERQUE, NM.
October 5, 1968.

15. NEW HAVEN ARENA, CT.
October 11, 1968.

16. CHICAGO
October 23, 1968.

17. MEMORIAL AUDITORIUM, DALLAS
October 25, 1968.

18. MADISON SQUARE GARDEN, NEW YORK
November 2, 1968.

19. ROYAL ALBERT HALL, LONDON
November 26, 1968.

DEREK AND THE DOMINOS

1. MARQUEE, LONDON
September 11, 1970.

2. LYCEUM, LONDON
October 11, 1970.

3. FILLMORE EAST, NEW YORK
October 24, 1970.

4. LUDLOW'S GARAGE, CINCINNATI
October 1970.

5. McFARLIN AUDITORIUM, DALLAS
November 6, 1970.

6. PAINTER'S MILL, BALTIMORE
November 14, 1970.

7. MEMORIAL AUDITORIUM, SACRAMENTO
November 17, 1970.

8. SANTA MONICA AUDITORIUM, WITH DELANEY BRAMLETT
November 20, 1970.

9. CURTIS HICKSON HALL, TAMPA, WITH DUANE ALLMAN
December 1, 1970.

10. CAPITOL THEATRE, PORT CHESTER
December 5, 1970.

11. SUFFOLK COLLEGE, NEW YORK
December 6, 1970.

12. JOHNNY CASH TV SHOW
November 5, 1970.

ERIC CLAPTON

1. RAINBOW, LONDON
January 13, 1973 (1st show).

2. RAINBOW, LONDON
January 13, 1973 (2nd show).

3. YALE BOWL, NEW HAVEN
June 28, 1974.

4. SPECTRUM, PHILADELPHIA
June 29, 1974.

5. NASSAU COLISEUM, LONG ISLAND, NEW YORK
June 30, 1974.

6. INTERNATIONAL AMPHITHEATRE, CHICAGO
July 2, 1974.

7. MUSIC PARK, COLUMBUS
July 4, 1974.

8. THREE RIVERS STADIUM, PITTSBURGH
July 5, 1974.

9. WAR MEMORIAL STADIUM, BUFFALO
July 6, 1974.
Jam with Freddie King.

10. ROOSEVELT STADIUM, JERSEY CITY
July 7, 1974.
Jam with Freddie King.

11. THE FORUM, MONTREAL
July 9, 1974.

12. CIVIC CENTRE, PROVIDENCE
July 10, 1974.

13. BOSTON GARDENS, BOSTON
July 12, 1974.

14. MADISON SQUARE GARDEN, NEW YORK
July 13, 1974.
Jam with Todd Rungren.

15. CAPITOL CENTRE, LARGO
July 14, 1974.

16. LONG BEACH ARENA, LOS ANGELES
July 19, 1974.

17. LONG BEACH ARENA, LOS ANGELES
July 20, 1974.

18. COW PALACE, SAN FRANCISCO
July 21, 1974.

19. COLISEUM, DENVER
July 23, 1974.

20. COLISEUM, DENVER
July 24, 1974.

21. OMNI, ATLANTA
August 1, 1974.
Jam with Pete Townshend.

22. COLISEUM, GREENSBORO
August 2, 1974.
Jam with Pete Townshend.

23. WEST PALM BEACH, MIAMI
August 4, 1974.
Jam with Keith Moon, Joe Walsh, Pete Townshend.

24. THE SPECTRUM, PHILADELPHIA
October 6, 1974.

25. PALAIS DES SPORTS, PARIS
December 2, 1974.

26. HAMMERSMITH ODEON, LONDON
December 4, 1974.

27. HAMMERSMITH ODEON, LONDON
December 5, 1974.
Jam with Ronnie Wood.

28. TAMPA STADIUM
June 16, 1975.

29. CONVENTION CENTRE, NIAGARA FALLS
June 23, 1975.
Jam with Santana.

30. CIVIC CENTRE, PROVIDENCE
June 25, 1975.
Jam with Santana.

31. NASSAU COLISEUM, LONG ISLAND, NEW YORK
June 28, 1975.
Jam with Santana, John McLaughlin.

32. DANE COUNTY, MADISON
July 8, 1975.
Jam with Santana.

33. KIEL AUDITORIUM, ST. LOUIS
July 11, 1975.
Jam with Santana.

34. STANFORD UNIVERSITY
August 9, 1975.
Jam with Santana.

35. L.A.FORUM, LOS ANGELES
August 14, 1975.
Jam with Keith Moon, Joe Cocker, Santana.

36. SWING AUDITORIUM, SAN BERNADINO
August 15, 1975.
Jam with Jerry McGhee, Santana.

37. MADISON SQUARE GARDEN, NEW YORK
June 22, 1975.
Jam with Rolling Stones on 'Sympathy For The Devil'.

38. THE SCOPE, NORFOLK, VIRGINIA
August 30, 1975.
Jam with Poco.

39. CRYSTAL PALACE, LONDON
July 31, 1976.
Jam with Larry Coryell, Freddie King, Ronnie Wood.

40. BBC TV THEATRE, SHEPHERDS BUSH, LONDON
April 26, 1977.

41. HAMMERSMITH ODEON, LONDON
April 27, 1977.

42. HAMMERSMITH ODEON, LONDON
April 28, 1977.
Jam with Ronnie Lane.

43. RAINBOW, LONDON
April 29, 1977.
Jam with Pete Townshend.

44. FALCONER THEATRE, COPENHAGEN
June 9, 1977.

45. VORST NATIONAL, BRUSSELS
June 13, 1977.

46. PAVILLON DE PARIS, PARIS
June 14, 1977.

47. KOSEIKIN HALL, OSAKA, JAPAN
October 1, 1977.

48. CLUB JUVENTUS, BARCELONA
November 6, 1978.

49. PALAIS DES SPORTS, LYON
November 8, 1978.

50. FESTHALLE, FRANKFURT
November 11, 1978.

51. PHILIPSHALLE, DUSSELDORF
November 14, 1978.
Jam with Muddy Waters.

52. PAVILLON DE PARIS
November 18, 1978.

53. VORST NATIONAL, BRUSSELS
November 19, 1978.

54. APOLLO, GLASGOW
November 24, 1978.

55. HAMMERSMITH ODEON, LONDON
December 5, 1978.
Jam with Muddy Waters.

56. HAMMERSMITH ODEON, LONDON
December 6, 1978.

57. CIVIC HALL, GUILDFORD
December 7, 1978.
Jam with Muddy Waters, Elton John, George Harrison.

58. COBO ARENA, DETROIT
March 28. 1978.

59. NASSAU COLISEUM, LONG ISLAND, NEW YORK
April 3, 1978.

60. FEYENORD STADIUM, ROTTERDAM
June 23, 1978.

61. ZEPPELINFIELD, NUREMBURG
July 1, 1978.

62. BLACKBUSH, CAMBERLEY, SURREY
June 15, 1978.

63. NATIONAL STADIUM, DUBLIN
March 17, 1979.

64. THE SPECTRUM, PHILADELPHIA
April 4, 1979.

65. OMNI AUDITORIUM, ATLANTA
April 21, 1979.

66. CAPITOL CENTRE, WASHINGTON
April 26. 1979.

67. RICHFIELD COLISEUM, CLEVELAND
June 2, 1979.

68. CITY HALL, NEWCASTLE
May 7, 1980.

69. HAMMERSMITH ODEON, LONDON
May 15, 1980.

70. HAMMERSMITH ODEON, LONDON
May 16, 1980.

71. HAMMERSMITH ODEON, LONDON
May 17, 1980.

72. CIVIC HALL, GUILDFORD, SURREY
May 18, 1980.
Jam with Jeff Beck.

73. RAINBOW, LONDON
February 5, 1981.

74. PARAMOUNT THEATRE, SEATTLE
March 5, 1981.

75. PARAMOUNT THEATRE, SEATTLE
March 6, 1981.

76. PARAMOUNT THEATRE, SEATTLE
March 7, 1981.

77. DANE COUNTY EXPO. CENTRE, MADISON
March 13, 1981.

78. THEATRE ROYAL, DRURY

THE LIVE TAPES

LANE, LONDON
September 9, 1981.

79. THEATRE ROYAL, DRURY LANE
September 10, 1981.

80. THEATRE ROYAL, DRURY LANE
September 12, 1981.

81. THE ISSTADION, STOCKHOLM
October 9, 1981.

82. RANDERSHALLE, RANDERS, DENMARK
October 17, 1981.

83. CIVIC HALL, WOLVERHAMPTON
November 16, 1981.

84. SPORTATORIUM, HOLLYWOOD, FLORIDA
June 30, 1982.
Jam with Muddy Waters.

85. PARAMOUNT THEATRE, SEATTLE
February 1, 1983.

86. PARAMOUNT THEATRE, SEATTLE
February 2, 1983.

87. CONVENTION CENTRE, SACRAMENTO
February 6, 1983.

88. COW PALACE, SAN FRANCISCO
February 7, 1983.

89. UNIVERSAL AMPHITHEATRE, L.A.
February 8, 1983.

90. LONG BEACH ARENA, LOS ANGELES
February 9, 1983.

91. SPECIAL EVENTS CENTRE, AUSTIN
February 13, 1983.

92. REUNION ARENA, DALLAS
February 15, 1983.

93. KIEL AUDITORIUM, ST. LOUIS
February 18, 1983.

94. THE SPECTRUM, PHILADELPHIA
February 21, 1983.
Jam with Ry Cooder.

95. WORCESTER, MASSACHUSETTS
March 1, 1983.

96. PLAYHOUSE, EDINBURGH
April 8, 1983.

97. PLAYHOUSE, EDINBURGH
April 9, 1983.

98. CITY HALL, NEWCASTLE
April 11, 1983.

99. EMPIRE, LIVERPOOL
April 12, 1983.

100. NATIONAL STADIUM, DUBLIN
April 14, 1983.

101. NATIONAL STADIUM, DUBLIN
April 15, 1983.

102. NATIONAL STADIUM, DUBLIN
April 16, 1983.

103. STADTHALLE, BREMEN
April 20, 1983.

104. GRUGAHALLE, ESSEN
April 21, 1983.

105. AHOY HALL, ROTTERDAM
April 23, 1983.

106. CHAPITEAU DE PANTIN, PARIS
April 24, 1983.

107. SPORTHALLE, COLOGNE
April 26, 1983.

108. FESTHALLE, FRANKFURT
April 27, 1983.

109. RHEIN NECKAR HALLE, EPPELHEIM
April 29, 1983.

1 10. ST. AUSTELL COLISEUM
May 13, 1983.

111. POOLE ARTS CENTRE
May 14, 1983.

112. HAMMERSMITH ODEON, LONDON
May 16, 1983.

113. HAMMERSMITH ODEON, LONDON
May 17, 1983.

114. HAMMERSMITH ODEON, LONDON
May 18, 1983.

115. HAMMERSMITH ODEON, LONDON
May 19, 1983.

116. APOLLO THEATRE, MANCHESTER
May 21, 1983.

117. DE MONTFORT HALL, LEICESTER
May 22, 1983.

118. CIVIC HALL, GUILDFORD
May 24, 1983.
Jam with Jimmy Page, Phil Collins, Paul Brady, Chas & Dave.

119. NEW VICTORIA PALACE, LONDON
June 5, 1983.

120. KINGSWOOD MUSIC THEATRE, TORONTO
July 25, 1983.

121. RED ROCKS, DENVER
July 16, 1983.

122. RED ROCKS, DENVER
July 17, 1983.
Jam with The Blasters.

**123. ROYAL ALBERT HALL,
LONDON**
September 20, 1983.

**124. ROYAL ALBERT HALL,
LONDON**
September 21, 1983.

125. REUNION ARENA, DALLAS
November 28, 1983.

126. REUNION ARENA, DALLAS
November 29, 1983.

**127. COW PALACE, SAN
FRANCISCO**
December 1, 1983.

**128. COW PALACE, SAN
FRANCISCO**
December 2, 1983.

**129. COW PALACE, SAN
FRANCISCO**
December 3, 1983.

130. L.A. FORUM, LOS ANGELES
December 5, 1983.

131. L.A. FORUM, LOS ANGELES
December 6, 1983.

**132. MADISON SQUARE GARDEN,
NEW YORK**
December 8, 1983.

**133. MADISON SQUARE GARDEN,
NEW YORK**
December 9, 1983.

123 to 133 are the ARMS concerts which featured Eric Clapton, Jimmy Page and Jeff Beck playing together for the first time. Ronnie Wood also joined them for the last two nights in New York.